# QUICK SHORT
# CHICKEN
## RECIPES

### The Confident Cooking Promise of Success

Welcome to the world of Confident Cooking, where recipes are double-tested by our team of home economists to achieve a high standard of success—and delicious results every time.

bay books

# C O N T E

Easy chicken salad, page 29

Chicken bagel burger, page 21

| | | | |
|---|---|---|---|
| Cooking hints and tips | 4 | Barbecues and grills | 48 |
| Soups for all occasions | 6 | Marinades and glazes | 58 |
| Light meals and salads | 18 | Everyday family meals | 66 |
| Sandwich and jaffle fillings | 26 | Special occasion dining | 94 |
| Stir-fries and pan-fries | 34 | Index and glossary | 111–112 |

Tortilla soup, page 10

Chicken salad with honey-glazed sweet potato, page 20

# N T S

Chicken and feta salad, page 33

Chicken and artichoke pizza, page 69

The Publisher thanks the following for their assistance in the photography: Chief Australia, Sunbeam Corporation, Kambrook, Sheldon & Hammond, Southcorp Appliances, Bertoli Olive Oil, Hale Imports, Shack, Tatti.

**Front cover:** Chicken breast stuffed with spinach and feta, page 105
**Inside front cover:** Coq au vin, page 95
**Back cover:** Chicken salad with honey-glazed sweet potato, page 20

Peppered chicken stir-fry, page 40

Smoked chicken and corn fritters, page 32

All recipes are double-tested by our team of home economists. When we test our recipes, we rate them for ease of preparation. The following cookery ratings are on the recipes in this book, making them easy to use and understand.

A single Cooking with Confidence symbol indicates a recipe that is simple and generally quick to make —perfect for beginners.

Two symbols indicate the need for just a little more care and a little more time.

Three symbols indicate special dishes that need more investment in time, care and patience—but the results are worth it.

### IMPORTANT
Those who might be at risk from the effects of salmonella food poisoning (the elderly, pregnant women, young children and those suffering from immune deficiency diseases) should consult their doctor with any concerns about eating raw eggs.

# COOKING HINTS AND TIPS

Chicken is a versatile and affordable food and lends itself to many different recipes and styles of cooking. It is also a good source of protein and minerals such as potassium and phosphorus and, without its skin, is very low in fat.

### BUYING AND STORING CHICKEN

When buying chicken, look for pieces with flesh that looks light pink and moist and is free of blemishes and bruises. Free-range and corn-fed chickens are available from speciality poultry shops and, while generally smaller and more expensive, tend to have a better flavour and texture than intensively farmed chickens.

Whole chickens are sold by a number that relates to their weight. For example, a No. 14 chicken weighs 1.4 kg (3 lb 2 oz), a No. 15 chicken weighs 1.5 kg (3 lb 5 oz). As a general rule, a No. 15 chicken will serve 4 people.

Try to buy chicken last when you are out shopping to minimize the amount of time it is out of the refrigerator. If you are buying a frozen chicken, make sure it is frozen solid and tightly wrapped. If it has even slightly defrosted, do not try to refreeze it as this can promote the growth of harmful bacteria. Continue to defrost it on a tray on the bottom shelf of the refrigerator where it cannot drip onto any other foods. Thawed

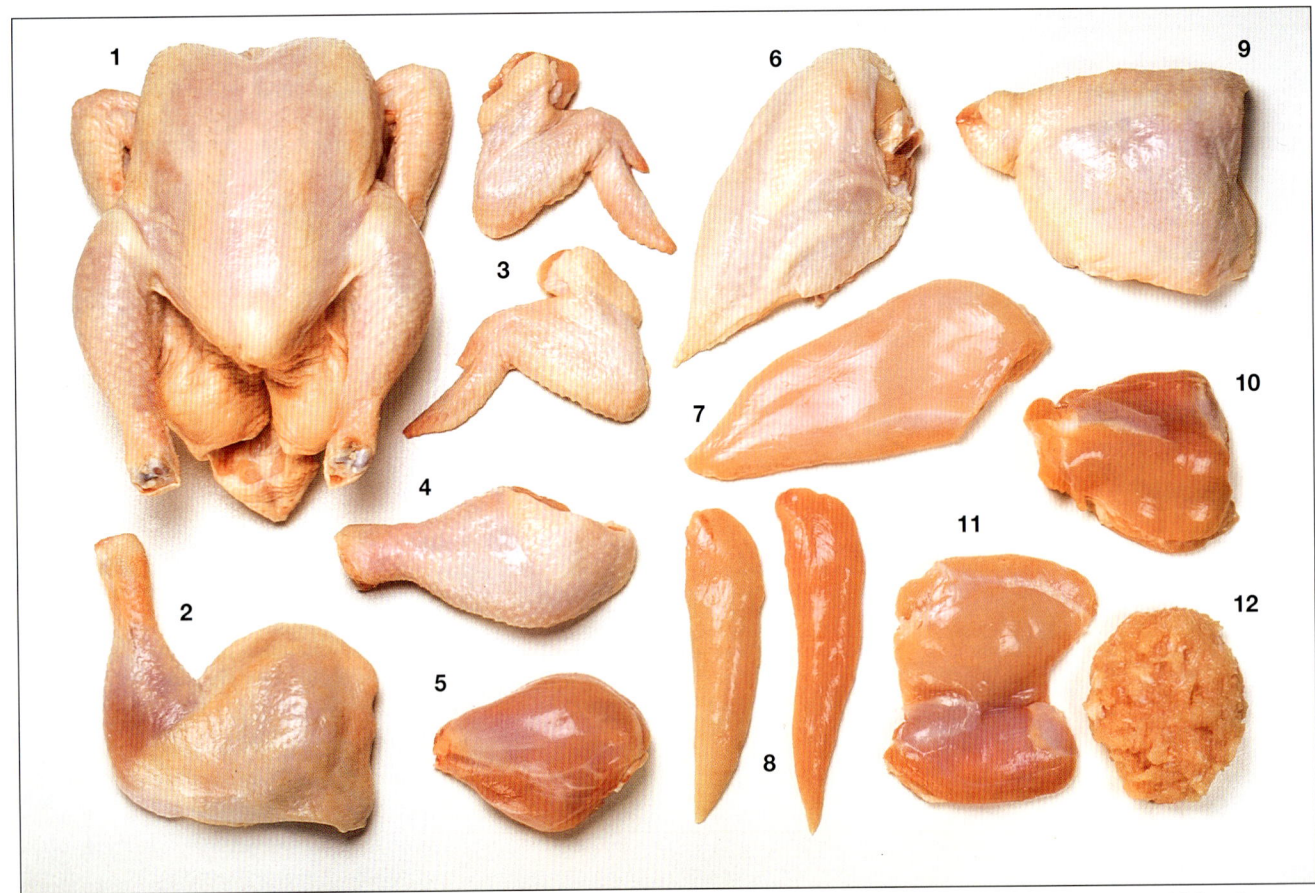

*1. whole chicken 2. Maryland (leg quarter) 3. chicken wings 4. drumstick 5. lovely legs 6. chicken breast on the bone 7. chicken breast fillet 8. tenderloins 9. chicken thigh piece 10. skinless thigh cutlet 11. chicken thigh fillet 12. minced (ground) chicken*

chicken should be cooked within 12 hours and must never be refrozen.

Fresh chicken should be taken out of its packaging, covered loosely with foil or plastic wrap and kept on a plate in the bottom of the refrigerator where it cannot drip onto any other food. Fresh chicken should be used within 2 days, or, alternatively, frozen for up to 8–12 months. When freezing, be sure to expel all the air from the freezer bag before sealing.

### DEFROSTING CHICKEN

| | |
|---|---|
| 1 kg (2 lb 4 oz): 13 hours | 2.5 kg (5 lb 8 oz): 20 hours |
| 1.5 kg (3 lb 5 oz): 15 hours | 3 kg (6 lb 8 oz): 24 hours |
| 2 kg (4 lb 8 oz): 17 hours | 3.5 kg (7 lb 10 oz): 28 hours |

Whole chickens should be defrosted in the refrigerator. Chicken pieces can be defrosted in the microwave (with the thickest portions to the outside of the plate), but don't defrost whole chickens in the microwave, as they will defrost unevenly and some parts may start to cook while others remain frozen. Never defrost chicken at room temperature and never thaw under running water. Bacteria such as salmonella can be activated if a defrosting chicken gets too warm. And it must be fully thawed before cooking begins. Of course, you can also buy pre-cooked barbecue chicken.

*Defrost chicken pieces in the microwave with the thickest part on the outside.*

## CHICKEN STOCK

There are plenty of good-quality ready-made chicken stocks or stock cubes available, and chicken consommé can usually be used as a substitute. However, nothing really beats the flavour of a homemade stock. Chicken bones can be bought from a butcher or chicken shop and the neck and giblets of roasting chickens can be added as well. You can also use chicken wings.

To make chicken stock, put 2 kg (4 lb 8 oz) chicken bones or wings, 2 quartered, unpeeled onions, 2 chopped, unpeeled carrots, 2 chopped celery sticks, including leaves, and 3.5 litres (14 cups) of water in a large saucepan. Bring slowly to the boil.

*Skim any scum off the surface of the stock during the cooking process.*

Skim any scum off the surface as required and add 1 bouquet garni (a bay leaf and sprigs of parsley, thyme and marjoram tied together with string) and 12 black peppercorns. Reduce the heat and simmer gently for 3 hours, skimming the surface regularly. Ladle

*Remove the solids from the stock using a sieve placed over a bowl.*

the stock in batches into a fine sieve over a bowl. Gently press the solids with the ladle to extract all the liquid. Let the stock cool, then refrigerate until cold and spoon off any fat from the top. At this stage you can reduce the stock to concentrate its flavour (dilute before using) and store in the refrigerator for up to 2 days or in the freezer for up to 8–12 months. Makes 2.5 litres (10 cups).

## TIME SAVERS

There are few things more irritating or wasteful than using a tablespoon of herbs or tomato paste (purée) in a recipe and having to throw the rest away unused. If you only need a small amount, you can freeze the rest in small, convenient portions to be used at a later date.

**Freezing stock** — Put a freezer bag into a measuring jug and pour the stock into the bag to get 250 ml (1 cup) stock. Seal tightly and freeze.

**Leftover herbs** — Finely chop any leftover herbs and wrap 1 tablespoon measurements in plastic wrap. Seal and freeze.

**Breadcrumbs** — When a recipe asks for fresh breadcrumbs, make extra and put the leftovers in freezer bags. Make sure all the air is expelled and seal tightly. Label with a date and the quantity.

**Ginger** — Fresh ginger can be kept wrapped in foil in the refrigerator or, for longer storage, cut into small pieces, wrapped tightly in plastic wrap and frozen.

**Tomato paste (purée)** — Spoon tomato paste into ice-cube trays and freeze. Once frozen, store in freezer bags.

**Fresh herbs** — Herbs such as chives, parsley, mint, basil and coriander (cilantro) grow easily in the garden or in pots on the kitchen window sill. Simply pick them as you need them.

*Freeze tomato paste, stock and herbs in small, convenient portions.*

# SOUPS FOR ALL OCCASIONS

## ASIAN CHICKEN NOODLE SOUP

Preparation time: 10 minutes
Total cooking time: 10 minutes
Serves 4

85 g (3 oz) fresh egg noodles
1.25 litres (5 cups) chicken stock
1 tablespoon mirin (see Note)
2 tablespoons soy sauce
3 cm (1¼ inch) piece fresh ginger, peeled and julienned
2 chicken breast fillets, thinly sliced
2 bunches baby bok choy (pak choi), stalks trimmed, leaves separated
coriander (cilantro) leaves, to garnish

**1** Soak the noodles in boiling water for 1 minute, drain and set aside. In a large saucepan, heat the stock to simmering, add the mirin, soy sauce, ginger, chicken and noodles. Cook for 5 minutes, or until the chicken is tender and the noodles are warmed through. Remove any scum from the surface of the soup.

**2** Add the bok choy and cook for 2 minutes, or until the bok choy has wilted. Serve garnished with coriander. Serve with sweet chilli sauce, if desired.

**NUTRITION PER SERVE**
Protein 30 g; Fat 3 g; Carbohydrate 15 g; Dietary Fibre 1 g; Cholesterol 65 mg; 915 kJ (220 cal)

### COOK'S FILE

**Note:** Mirin is a sweet rice wine used for cooking. Sweet sherry, with a little sugar added, can be used instead.

## CHUNKY CHICKEN AND VEGETABLE SOUP

Preparation time: 15 minutes
Total cooking time: 15 minutes
Serves 4

1 tablespoon oil
1 carrot, sliced
1 leek, chopped
2 chicken thigh fillets,
　cut into 2 cm (³/₄ inch) pieces
35 g (¹/₄ cup) ditalini pasta
1 litre (4 cups) vegetable stock
2 ripe tomatoes, diced

**1** Heat the oil in a saucepan and cook the carrot and leek over medium heat for 4 minutes, or until soft. Add the chicken and cook for a further 2 minutes, or until the chicken has changed colour.

**2** Add the pasta and the vegetable stock, cover and bring to the boil. Reduce the heat and simmer for 10 minutes, or until the pasta is cooked. Add the tomato halfway through the cooking. Season to taste with salt and freshly ground black pepper. Serve with fresh crusty bread.

**NUTRITION PER SERVE**
Protein 20 g; Fat 7 g; Carbohydrate 9 g; Dietary Fibre 2 g; Cholesterol 40 mg; 725 kJ (173 cal)

### COOK'S FILE

**Note:** Ditalini pasta can be replaced with any small soup pasta.

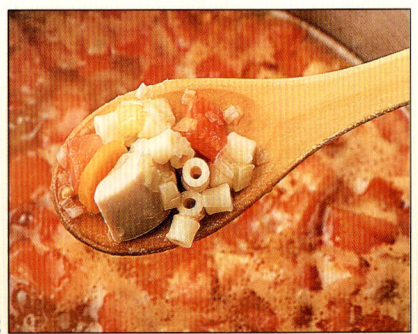

## CHILLI COCONUT CHICKEN SOUP

Preparation time: 10 minutes
Total cooking time: 10 minutes
Serves 4

60 ml (¼ cup) oil
2 cm (¾ inch) piece fresh ginger, peeled and grated
6 spring onions (scallions), sliced into 3 cm (1¼ inch) lengths
6 chicken breast fillets, thinly sliced
80 ml (⅓ cup) sweet chilli sauce
500 ml (2 cups) coconut milk
2 tablespoons lime juice

**1** Heat the oil in a saucepan over high heat, add the ginger and spring onion and cook for 1 minute. Add the chicken and cook for 2–3 minutes, or until golden. Add the sweet chilli sauce and cook for a further 1 minute.
**2** Add 350 ml (1⅓ cups) water and the coconut milk. Bring to the boil, then reduce the heat and simmer for 4–5 minutes. Add the lime juice, season with salt and add a little more sweet chilli sauce, if desired. Serve with lime wedges.

**NUTRITION PER SERVE**
Protein 45 g; Fat 45 g; Carbohydrate 8.5 g; Dietary Fibre 3 g; Cholesterol 94 mg; 2558 kJ (610 cal)

### COOK'S FILE

**Note:** Try adding a little fish sauce at the end of cooking for extra flavour.

## TORTILLA SOUP

Preparation time: 10 minutes
Total cooking time: 15 minutes
Serves 4

4 corn tortillas (also sold as enchilada tortillas)
750 ml (3 cups) chicken stock
500 g (1 lb 2 oz) tomatoes, seeded and diced
1/4 teaspoon cayenne pepper
1 teaspoon ground cumin
1 large chicken breast fillet
15 g (1/2 cup) coriander (cilantro) leaves, shredded
1 avocado, peeled and diced

**1** Preheat the oven to 180°C (350°F/Gas 4). Cut the tortillas in half, stack the halves and cut into 1.5 cm (5/8 inch) wide strips. Spread the strips on a baking tray and bake, turning once, for 3–5 minutes, or until slightly crisp.

**2** Meanwhile, put the stock, tomato, cayenne pepper and cumin in a saucepan. Bring to the boil, then reduce the heat and simmer for 5 minutes. Cut the chicken into bite-sized pieces, add to the pan and simmer for 5 minutes, or until cooked through. Season to taste with salt and black pepper.

**3** Ladle the soup into four bowls. Sprinkle the coriander leaves and avocado over each bowl. Lay the tortilla strips across the bowl and serve immediately.

**NUTRITION PER SERVE**
Protein 35 g; Fat 20 g; Carbohydrate 60 g; Dietary Fibre 5.5 g; Cholesterol 50 mg; 2314 kJ (553 cal)

1

2

## CHICKEN AND MUSHROOM SOUP

Preparation time: 10 minutes
Total cooking time: 10 minutes
Serves 4

1½ tablespoons oil
2 teaspoons grated fresh ginger
4 spring onions (scallions), finely chopped
1 chicken breast fillet, cut into thin strips
100 g (3½ oz) button mushrooms, sliced
410 g (14 oz) can chicken consommé
50 g (1¾ oz) instant noodles
3 teaspoons kecap manis (see Note)

**1** Heat the oil in a saucepan, add the ginger, spring onion and chicken and stir-fry over high heat for 4–5 minutes, or until the chicken changes colour. Add the mushrooms and cook for a further 1 minute.

**2** Add the consommé and 500 ml (2 cups) water and bring to the boil. Stir in the noodles, then reduce the heat and simmer for 3 minutes, or until the noodles are soft. Stir in the kecap manis and serve.

**NUTRITION PER SERVE**
Protein 13 g; Fat 9 g; Carbohydrate 5 g; Dietary Fibre 1 g; Cholesterol 25 mg; 635 kJ (150 cal)

### COOK'S FILE

**Note:** Kecap manis is a thick, sweet sauce. If unavailable, use soy sauce sweetened with a little soft brown sugar.

## CHICKEN AND SWEET CORN SOUP

Preparation time: 10 minutes
Total cooking time: 20 minutes
Serves 4

1 tablespoon oil
2 bacon rashers, finely chopped
1 small onion, finely chopped
2 x 420 g (15 oz) cans creamed corn
750 ml (3 cups) chicken stock
2 chicken thigh fillets, cut into bite-sized pieces
2 tablespoons chopped dill

**1** Heat the oil in a large saucepan and cook the bacon and onion over medium heat for 5 minutes, or until the onion is soft.
**2** Add the corn and stock. Bring to the boil, then reduce the heat and simmer for 5 minutes. Add the chicken and dill and simmer for 5–10 minutes, or until the chicken is cooked through. Season and serve.

**NUTRITION PER SERVE**
Protein 25 g; Fat 9 g; Carbohydrate 35 g; Dietary Fibre 7.5 g; Cholesterol 45 mg; 1390 kJ (330 cal)

# CREAMY CHICKEN AND ZUCCHINI SOUP

Preparation time: 10 minutes
Total cooking time: 10 minutes
Serves 4

20 g (¾ oz) butter
3 chicken breast fillets, thinly sliced
800 g (1 lb 12 oz) zucchini (courgettes), grated
1 onion, grated
2 cloves garlic, crushed
2 tablespoons plain (all-purpose) flour
750 ml (3 cups) chicken stock
250 ml (1 cup) cream

**1** Melt the butter in a large saucepan, add the chicken and cook over medium heat for 1–2 minutes, or until the chicken changes colour. Add the zucchini, onion and garlic, and cook, stirring occasionally, for 5 minutes.

**2** Stir in the flour and cook for 1 minute. Add the stock, bring to the boil, stirring until it boils and thickens slightly. Reduce the heat and simmer for 1 minute. Stir in the cream and cook for 2 minutes. Season and serve.

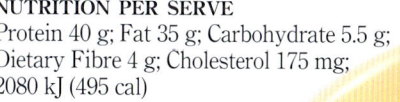

**NUTRITION PER SERVE**
Protein 40 g; Fat 35 g; Carbohydrate 5.5 g; Dietary Fibre 4 g; Cholesterol 175 mg; 2080 kJ (495 cal)

## CHICKEN, LEEK AND TOMATO SOUP

Preparation time: 10 minutes
Total cooking time: 12 minutes
Serves 4

60 g (2¼ oz) butter
3 leeks, thinly sliced
3 chicken breast fillets
750 ml (3 cups) chicken stock
2 cloves garlic, crushed
425 g (15 oz) can crushed tomatoes
¼ teaspoon soft brown sugar
1 tablespoon chopped basil leaves
chopped basil, extra, to garnish

**1** Melt the butter in a large saucepan over medium heat, add the leek and cook for 2 minutes without browning.
**2** Halve the chicken breast fillets lengthways and thinly slice them. Increase the heat, add the chicken to the saucepan and cook for 3 minutes, or until the chicken is browned.
**3** Add the stock, garlic, tomato, sugar and basil. Bring to the boil, then reduce the heat and simmer for 5–6 minutes, or until the chicken is tender. Season and garnish with extra fresh basil. Serve with crusty bread.

NUTRITION PER SERVE
Protein 35 g; Fat 15 g; Carbohydrate 7 g; Dietary Fibre 3.5 g; Cholesterol 115 mg; 1350 kJ (325 cal)

### COOK'S FILE

**Variation:** Try adding beans or lentils for a heartier soup.

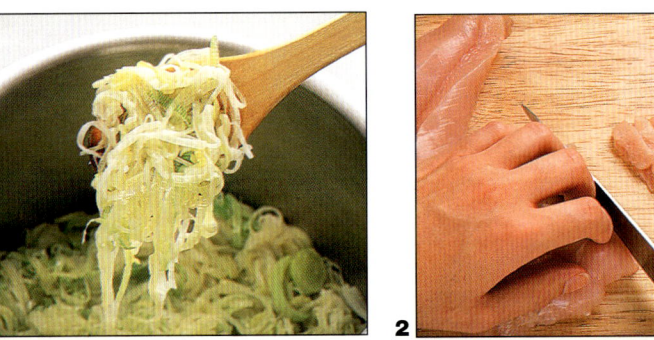

## CREAM OF CHICKEN SOUP

Preparation time: 10 minutes
Total cooking time: 12 minutes
Serves 4

60 g (2¼ oz) butter
1 onion, finely chopped
2 cloves garlic, crushed
1 teaspoon finely chopped thyme
60 g (½ cup) plain (all-purpose) flour
1 litre (4 cups) chicken stock
1 chicken breast fillet, thinly sliced
60 ml (¼ cup) cream
thyme, extra, to garnish

**1** Melt the butter in a saucepan, add the onion and cook over medium heat for 2–3 minutes, or until soft. Add the garlic and thyme and cook for 2 minutes. Add the flour and cook, stirring, for 1 minute.

**2** Remove the pan from the heat and gradually stir in the stock. Return to the heat, add the chicken and stir constantly for 3–4 minutes, or until the soup boils and thickens. Reduce the heat, add the cream, and simmer for 2 minutes. Season and serve sprinkled with extra thyme.

**NUTRITION PER SERVE**
Protein 16 g; Fat 20 g; Carbohydrate 15 g; Dietary Fibre 1 g; Cholesterol 90 mg; 1270 kJ (305 cal)

## CHICKEN WONTON SOUP

Preparation time: 20 minutes
Total cooking time: 10 minutes
Serves 4–6

175 g (6 oz) minced (ground) chicken
1 tablespoon finely chopped coriander (cilantro) leaves
30 gow gee wrappers (see Note)
410 g (14 oz) can chicken consommé
5 cm (2 inch) piece fresh ginger, peeled and julienned
1 tablespoon salt-reduced soy sauce
2 teaspoons mirin
8 spring onions (scallions), sliced on the diagonal
1 tablespoon chopped coriander (cilantro) leaves, extra

**1** Combine the minced chicken and coriander in a bowl and season generously with salt and pepper. Place 1 teaspoon of the mixture just off centre on a gow gee wrapper, moisten the edge with water and fold in half, covering the filling, to form a half circle. Repeat with all of the mixture. Cover the wontons with a damp tea towel to prevent them from drying out.
**2** In a large saucepan, combine the consommé with 1 litre (4 cups) water. Bring slowly to the boil, then reduce the heat and simmer for 1 minute. Add the ginger, soy sauce and mirin, and simmer for a further 2 minutes.
**3** Gently lower the wontons into the soup, in batches, and simmer for 3–5 minutes, or until they are cooked. Return the wontons to the pan and stir in the spring onion. Serve sprinkled with the extra coriander.

**NUTRITION PER SERVE (6)**
Protein 8 g; Fat 1 g; Carbohydrate 6 g; Dietary Fibre 0.5 g; Cholesterol 16 mg; 128 kJ (65 cal)

### COOK'S FILE

**Note:** Gow gee wrappers are made from egg pasta or egg noodle dough.

## CANJA (PORTUGUESE CHICKEN BROTH WITH RICE)

Preparation time: 15 minutes
Total cooking time: 1 hour
Serves 6

2.5 litres (10 cups) chicken stock
1 onion, cut into thin wedges
1 teaspoon grated lemon zest
1 mint sprig
500 g (1 lb 2 oz) potatoes, chopped
1 tablespoon olive oil
2 chicken breast fillets
200 g (1 cup) long-grain rice
2 tablespoons lemon juice
shredded mint, extra, to garnish

**1** Combine the chicken stock, onion, lemon zest, mint, potato and olive oil in a large saucepan. Slowly bring to the boil, then reduce the heat, add the chicken breasts and simmer gently for 20–25 minutes, or until the chicken is cooked through.
**2** Remove the chicken breast and discard the mint. Allow the chicken to cool, then cut it into thin slices.
**3** Meanwhile, add the rice to the pan and simmer for 25–30 minutes, or until the rice is tender. Return the sliced chicken to the pan, add the lemon juice and stir for 1–2 minutes, or until the chicken is warmed through. Season and serve garnished with mint.

**NUTRITION PER SERVE**
Protein 20 g; Fat 5 g; Carbohydrate 38 g; Dietary Fibre 2 g; Cholesterol 37 mg; 1197 kJ (286 cal)

### COOK'S FILE

**Note:** Rice and potato absorb liquid on standing, so serve immediately.

# LIGHT MEALS AND SALADS

## CHICKEN SANDWICHES WITH LEMON MAYONNAISE

Preparation time: 15 minutes
Total cooking time: 10 minutes
Serves 4

1 tablespoon oil
2 chicken breast fillets
1 Lebanese (short) cucumber
100 g (3½ oz) whole-egg mayonnaise
1 teaspoon finely grated lemon zest
1 tablespoon fresh lemon juice
1 loaf wood-fired sourdough or rye bread
30 g (1 cup) watercress leaves

**1** Heat the oil in a frying pan over medium heat, add the chicken and cook for 3–4 minutes on each side, or until cooked through. Leave to cool. When cold, shred the chicken into long strips. Thinly slice the cucumber. Combine the mayonnaise, lemon zest and lemon juice in a bowl.

**2** Slice 8 slices from the sourdough loaf and spread 4 slices with the lemon mayonnaise. Add the watercress leaves, cucumber and chicken. Season with salt and ground black pepper and top with the remaining slices of bread.

**NUTRITION PER SERVE**
Protein 30 g; Fat 17 g; Carbohydrate 25 g; Dietary Fibre 2.5 g; Cholesterol 70 mg; 1604 kJ (385 Cal)

## CHICKEN SALAD WITH HONEY-GLAZED SWEET POTATO

Preparation time: 15 minutes
Total cooking time: 30 minutes
Serves 4

1.2 kg (2 lb 11 oz) orange sweet potato, peeled and sliced
1 tablespoon honey
1 tablespoon oil
4 chicken breast fillets
2–3 tablespoons lemon juice
2 tablespoons olive oil
160 g (5½ oz) baby English spinach leaves
200 g (7 oz) feta cheese, diced

**1** Preheat the oven to 200°C (400°F/Gas 6). Place the sweet potato on a baking tray. Drizzle with the combined honey and oil to coat well and roast for 20 minutes, or until soft.
**2** Heat a non-stick frying pan over medium heat, add the chicken breasts and cook for 3–4 minutes each side, or until cooked through. Alternatively, sear the breasts and then place in the oven with the sweet potato for 10 minutes, or until cooked through. Leave to cool slightly and then slice into thin strips across the grain.
**3** Mix together the lemon juice and olive oil to make the dressing. Place the spinach leaves in a bowl, add the sweet potato, feta and chicken, and season. Pour the dressing over the salad, toss to coat the leaves and serve.

**NUTRITION PER SERVE**
Protein 70 g; Fat 30 g; Carbohydrate 55 g; Dietary Fibre 6.5 g; Cholesterol 155 mg; 3303 kJ (790 Cal)

### COOK'S FILE

**Note:** The sweet potato and the chicken can be cooked ahead of time and all the ingredients tossed together when you are ready to eat.

## CHICKEN BAGEL BURGER

Preparation time: 15 minutes
Total cooking time: 10 minutes
Serves 4

1 tablespoon oil
2 chicken breast fillets
2 ripe tomatoes, cut into 8 slices
4 slices Swiss cheese
2 tablespoons tomato relish
160 g ($^2/_3$ cup) whole-egg mayonnaise
4 poppy-seed bagels, halved
80 g ($2^1/_2$ oz) baby English spinach leaves
300 g ($10^1/_2$ oz) mixed antipasto vegetables from your delicatessen

**1** Heat the oil in a non-stick frying pan over medium heat and cook the chicken for 3–4 minutes each side, or until cooked through. Remove and keep warm. In the same pan, seal the tomato slices on each side. While still hot, cut each chicken breast in half through the centre. Place a slice of cheese on two halves and top with the other two halves to melt the cheese slightly. Cut the chicken breasts in half to give four cheese-filled pieces.
**2** Combine the tomato relish and the mayonnaise in a small bowl.
**3** To assemble the burgers, spread both halves of the bagel with the tomato relish mayonnaise, top with the spinach leaves, chicken breast, tomato slice and antipasto vegetables. Put the bagel lid on top and serve the burgers immediately.

**NUTRITION PER SERVE**
Protein 38 g; Fat 27 g; Carbohydrate 44 g; Dietary Fibre 5 g; Cholesterol 82 mg; 2393 kJ (572 Cal)

### COOK'S FILE

**Note:** The tomato relish mayonnaise can be made in advance and kept refrigerated for up to 1 week.

## SPICY CHICKEN PATTIES

Preparation time: 10 minutes + chilling
Total cooking time: 15 minutes
Serves 4

500 g (1 lb 2 oz) minced (ground) chicken
4 spring onions (scallions), finely chopped
20 g (1/3 cup) finely chopped coriander (cilantro) leaves
2 cloves garlic, crushed
3/4 teaspoon cayenne pepper
1 egg white, lightly beaten
2 tablespoons oil
1 lemon, halved

**1** Mix together all the ingredients except the oil and lemon, season with salt and freshly ground black pepper and shape the mixture into four patties. Refrigerate the patties for 20 minutes before cooking.

**2** Heat the oil in a large frying pan over medium heat, add the patties and cook for about 5 minutes on each side, or until browned and cooked through.

**3** Squeeze the lemon on the cooked patties and serve with a salad or use to make burgers.

**NUTRITION PER SERVE**
Protein 25 g; Fat 12 g; Carbohydrate 1 g; Dietary Fibre 1 g; Cholesterol 105 mg; 895 kJ (215 Cal)

## LIGHT MEALS AND SALADS

### VIETNAMESE-STYLE CHICKEN AND CABBAGE SALAD

Preparation time: 15 minutes
Total cooking time: 10 minutes
Serves 4

3 chicken breast fillets
1 red chilli, seeded, membrane removed, finely chopped
60 ml (¼ cup) lime juice
2 tablespoons soft brown sugar
60 ml (¼ cup) fish sauce
½ Chinese cabbage, shredded
2 carrots, grated
50 g (1 cup) shredded mint

**1** Put the chicken in a saucepan, cover with water and bring to the boil, then reduce the heat and simmer for 10 minutes, or until cooked through.
**2** While the chicken is cooking, mix together the chilli, lime juice, sugar and fish sauce. Remove the chicken from the water. Cool slightly, then shred into small pieces.
**3** Combine the chicken, cabbage, carrot, mint and dressing. Toss well and serve immediately.

**NUTRITION PER SERVE**
Protein 30 g; Fat 3 g; Carbohydrate 15 g; Dietary Fibre 3.5 g; Cholesterol 62 mg; 900 kJ (215 Cal)

### COOK'S FILE

**Hint:** Any leftovers can be used the next day in a stir-fry.

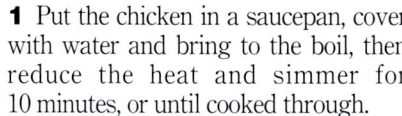

## CHICKEN CHICKPEA SALAD

Preparation time: 10 minutes
Total cooking time: 10 minutes
Serves 4

2 tablespoons extra virgin olive oil
2 large chicken breast fillets, sliced
400 g (14 oz) can chickpeas, drained
1 teaspoon seeded, chopped red chilli
2 cloves garlic, crushed
½ red onion, cut into wedges
1 tablespoon sherry vinegar or white wine vinegar
15 g (¼ cup) chopped mint
6 new potatoes, boiled and sliced

**1** Heat half the oil in a saucepan and cook the chicken over high heat for 5 minutes, or until browned and tender. Transfer to a bowl, cover and keep warm.
**2** Add the remaining oil, chickpeas, chilli and garlic to the pan. Cook for 5 minutes, or until the chickpeas are warmed through.
**3** Place the chickpeas in the bowl with the chicken and stir through the onion and vinegar. Toss through the mint leaves. Serve over the potatoes. Season with salt and black pepper.

NUTRITION PER SERVE
Protein 30 g; Fat 15 g; Carbohydrate 15 g; Dietary Fibre 5.5 g; Cholesterol 50 mg; 1275 kJ (305 Cal)

### COOK'S FILE

**Variation:** For a hotter dish, do not remove the seeds from the chilli.

# CHICKEN, BLUE CHEESE AND WALNUT SALAD

Preparation time: 15 minutes
Total cooking time: 20 minutes
Serves 4

2 large chicken breast fillets
80 ml ($^1/_3$ cup) olive oil
3 teaspoons dried French tarragon
60 g ($^1/_2$ cup) walnuts, chopped
2 tablespoons cider vinegar
1 teaspoon Dijon mustard
100 g ($3^1/_2$ oz) baby English spinach leaves
125 g ($4^1/_2$ oz) firm blue cheese, crumbled

**1** Preheat the oven to 170°C (325°F/Gas 3). Place the chicken breasts on a foil-lined baking tray. Brush with half the oil and sprinkle generously with freshly ground black pepper and 1 teaspoon dried tarragon. Cook under a hot griller (broiler) for 10 minutes, turning once. Meanwhile, place the walnuts on an oven tray and roast for 10 minutes, or until lightly golden.
**2** To make the dressing, whisk together the remaining tarragon, vinegar and Dijon mustard with the remaining olive oil. Season to taste.
**3** Cut the chicken across the grain into 1.5 cm ($^5/_8$ inch) thick strips. Put the spinach, chicken, walnuts and blue cheese in a large serving bowl, add the dressing, toss and serve immediately.

**NUTRITION PER SERVE**
Protein 35 g; Fat 40 g; Carbohydrate 0.5 g; Dietary Fibre 1.5 g; Cholesterol 90 mg; 2200 kJ (525 Cal)

### COOK'S FILE

**Note:** The chicken can be increased to 4 breasts to serve as a light dinner.

1

2

3

# SANDWICH AND JAFFLE FILLINGS

### CREAMY CHICKEN AND CELERY

Combine 350 g (2 cups) chopped barbecue chicken, 80 g ($1/3$ cup) whole-egg mayonnaise, 2 tablespoons sweet chilli sauce, 4 finely chopped spring onions (scallions), 1 diced stick celery, 1 tablespoon finely chopped coriander (cilantro) leaves, salt and ground black pepper. Serve on four toasted bagel halves and sprinkle over some snowpea (mangetout) sprouts. Cover with the remaining bagel halves. Serves 4.

### CHICKEN WITH SEMI-DRIED TOMATO AND GRUYERE JAFFLE

Butter 8 slices of wholegrain bread on one side. Slice 250 g (9 oz) smoked chicken and divide among 4 slices of the bread, buttered-side-down. Top with 100 g ($3^1/2$ oz) sliced semi-dried (sun-blushed) tomato and 100 g ($3^1/2$ oz) Gruyère cheese. Season with salt and pepper. Place the remaining slices of bread on top, buttered-side-up and cook in a jaffle iron or sandwich maker for 3 minutes, or until golden brown. Serve immediately. Makes 4.

### LEBANESE CHICKEN

Spread 200 g (7 oz) hummus over four Lebanese bread rounds. Combine 200 g (7 oz) cooked chopped barbecue chicken, $1^1/2$ cups ready-made tabouli, 1 teaspoon lemon juice and $1/2$ sliced red onion (optional). Divide the mixture among the Lebanese bread, season with salt and freshly ground black pepper and roll up tightly. Cut in half on the diagonal and serve immediately. Serves 4.

### CHICKEN WITH CRANBERRY AND CAMEMBERT

Combine 70 g ($1/4$ cup) cranberry sauce, 4 finely chopped spring onions (scallions), salt and freshly ground black pepper. Butter 8 slices of Turkish bread on one side and divide 200 g (7 oz) thinly sliced processed chicken among 4 slices of bread, buttered-side up. Top with the cranberry mixture and divide 200 g (7 oz) sliced camembert among the slices. Place the remaining slices of bread on top, buttered-side down and cook in a sandwich maker for 3 minutes, or until golden brown. Serve immediately. Serves 4.

### MANGO CHICKEN

Combine 350 g (2 cups) chopped smoked chicken, 70 g ($1/4$ cup) mango chutney, 2 teaspoons lime juice, 90 g ($1/3$ cup) natural yoghurt, salt and black pepper. Divide the mixture down the centre of four large Lebanese bread rounds, top with rocket (arugula) leaves and roll up tightly. Cut each roll into three and serve immediately. Serves 4.

### CHICKEN AND CORN JAFFLE

Combine 200 g (7 oz) diced cooked chicken, 315 g (11 oz) can creamed corn, 60 g ($1/2$ cup) grated Cheddar cheese, salt and freshly ground black pepper. Butter 8 slices of bread on one side and divide the chicken mixture among 4 slices, buttered-side down. Place the remaining slices of bread on top, buttered-side up, and cook in a jaffle iron or sandwich maker for 3 minutes, or until golden brown. Serve immediately with lime wedges. Serves 4.

*Clockwise from top left: Creamy chicken and celery; Chicken with cranberry and camembert; Mango chicken; Chicken and corn jaffle; Lebanese chicken; Chicken, semi-dried tomato and Gruyère jaffle.*

## SMOKED CHICKEN CAESAR SALAD

Preparation time: 10 minutes
Total cooking time: nil
Serves 4

1 cos (romaine) lettuce, torn
250 g (9 oz) smoked chicken breast, thinly sliced
250 g (1 cup) whole-egg mayonnaise
4 anchovy fillets, drained, chopped, reserving 1 teaspoon oil
2 cloves garlic, crushed
2 tablespoons lemon juice
65 g ($2/3$ cup) shaved Parmesan cheese
25 g ($3/4$ cup) croutons

**1** Place the lettuce and chicken on four individual plates or in a large serving bowl.
**2** To make the dressing, combine the mayonnaise, anchovies, anchovy oil, garlic, lemon juice, 15 g ($1/2$ oz) of the shaved Parmesan, and freshly ground black pepper in a food processor and process until smooth.
**3** Drizzle the dressing over the salad. Scatter with the croutons and remaining shaved Parmesan and serve.

**NUTRITION PER SERVE**
Protein 17 g; Fat 30 g; Carbohydrate 16 g; Dietary Fibre 1 g; Cholesterol 57 mg; 1660 kJ (395 Cal)

### COOK'S FILE

**Note:** Any leftover dressing will keep in the refrigerator in an airtight container for 1 week.

# LIGHT MEALS AND SALADS

## EASY CHICKEN SALAD

Preparation time: 10 minutes
Total cooking time: 25 minutes
Serves 4

4 chicken breast fillets
3 tablespoons extra virgin olive oil
150 g (5½ oz) green beans
250 g (9 oz) cherry tomatoes, halved
1 large avocado, sliced
1 red onion, finely sliced
16 small black olives
1 tablespoon lemon juice

**1** Preheat the oven to 220°C (425°F/Gas 7). Brush the chicken with 1 tablespoon of the oil and place on a lined oven tray. Cover with foil and bake for 15–20 minutes, or until just cooked. Transfer to a plate and cover loosely with paper towels. Leave to cool but do not refrigerate.
**2** Bring a saucepan of water to the boil and cook the beans for 3–4 minutes, or until tender. Drain. Plunge into iced water and drain.
**3** Cut the chicken on the diagonal into 1 cm (½ inch) slices. Arrange the beans in a serving dish, or individual dishes, and top with the chicken, tomato, avocado, onion and olives.
**4** In a small bowl, whisk the remaining oil and lemon juice and season to taste. Drizzle over the salad and serve immediately.

**NUTRITION PER SERVE**
Protein 60 g; Fat 30 g; Carbohydrate 5 g; Dietary Fibre 4 g; Cholesterol 120 mg; 2158 kJ (515 Cal)

### COOK'S FILE

**Variation:** Shredded basil leaves can be added before serving.

## CHICKEN MOZZARELLA STACKS

Preparation time: 10 minutes
Total cooking time: 10 minutes
Serves 4

2 tablespoons chopped basil
1 clove garlic, crushed
60 ml (¼ cup) olive oil
4 chicken breast fillets, flattened
3 tablespoons seasoned plain (all-purpose) flour
2 ripe tomatoes, sliced
150 g (1 cup) grated mozzarella cheese
40 g (1½ oz) whole or sliced good-quality pitted black olives

**1** Combine the basil, garlic and half the oil in a bowl, and season to taste.
**2** Coat the chicken with the flour, shaking off any excess. Heat the remainder of the oil in a large non-stick frying pan and cook the chicken in batches for 3–4 minutes, or until golden, turning once during cooking.
**3** Place the chicken breasts on a griller (broiler) tray and top with the tomato. Spread with the basil mixture and top with the grated mozzarella and olives. Place under a hot griller (broiler) until the cheese has melted. Serve immediately on toasted foccacia.

NUTRITION PER SERVE
Protein 25 g; Fat 25 g; Carbohydrate 8 g; Dietary Fibre 1.5 g; Cholesterol 50 mg; 1445 kJ (345 Cal)

1

2

3

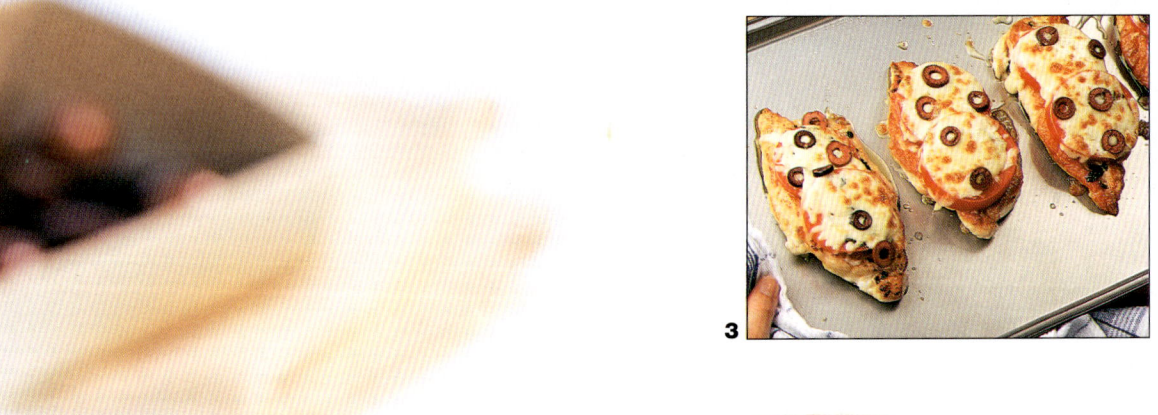

## LEBANESE CHICKEN ROLLS

Preparation time: 15 minutes
Total cooking time: nil
Makes 6

110 g (1/2 cup) prepared hummus
200 g (7 oz) plain yoghurt
8 spring onions (scallions), finely chopped
1/2 large barbecue chicken
3 large Lebanese flat-breads
2 butter lettuces, leaves separated
1 carrot, julienned
115 g (3/4 cup) chopped red capsicum (pepper)

**1** Mix together the hummus, plain yoghurt and spring onion.
**2** Remove the skin and bones from the chicken and cut the flesh into 1 cm (1/2 inch) cubes. Add the chicken to the hummus mixture, mix well and season with salt and pepper.
**3** Using a small sharp knife, split each flat-bread to make two thin rounds. Arrange the lettuce leaves over the flat-breads and top with the chicken mixture, carrot and capsicum. Roll up firmly, cut into thirds if desired and serve.

NUTRITION PER ROLL
Protein 20 g; Fat 8 g; Carbohydrate 35 g; Dietary Fibre 5 g; Cholesterol 40 mg; 1215 kJ (290 Cal)

## SMOKED CHICKEN AND CORN FRITTERS

Preparation time: 15 minutes
Total cooking time: 15 minutes
Serves 4

90 g (¾ cup) self-raising flour
1 egg, lightly beaten
170 ml (⅔ cup) milk
310 g (11 oz) can creamed corn
100 g (¾ cup) finely chopped smoked chicken
2 spring onions (scallions), sliced
1 tablespoon chopped chives
80 ml (⅓ cup) extra virgin olive oil

**1** Sift the flour into a large bowl. Make a well in the flour and add the egg and milk. Using a wooden spoon, gradually stir the mixture to form a smooth batter.
**2** Stir in the creamed corn, chicken, spring onion and chives. Season to taste with salt and freshly ground black pepper.
**3** Heat half the oil in a shallow non-stick frying pan and add heaped tablespoons of the batter, flattening the mixture out a little. Cook, in batches, over high heat for about 2 minutes each side, or until golden brown. Add the remaining oil during cooking when necessary. Drain the fritters on paper towels and serve immediately with pesto or olive tapenade, or a quick sauce made from plain yoghurt and mango or other fruit chutney.

**NUTRITION PER SERVE**
Protein 7 g; Fat 23 g; Carbohydrate 30 g; Dietary Fibre 3.5 g; Cholesterol 50 mg; 1475 kJ (355 Cal)

## CHICKEN AND FETA SALAD

Preparation time: 10 minutes
Total cooking time: nil
Serves 4–6

340 g (12 oz) jar artichokes marinated in oil
150 g (5½ oz) button mushrooms, sliced
100 g (3½ oz) semi-dried (sun-blushed) tomatoes
1 red onion, cut into rings
15 g (¼ cup) chopped basil
1 barbecue chicken
1 bunch rocket (arugula) leaves, trimmed
200 g (7 oz) feta cheese, cubed

**1** Place the artichokes and the oil marinade in a large bowl and add the mushrooms, tomato, onion and basil.
**2** Remove the skin and bones from the chicken and cut the flesh into bite-sized pieces. Add to the salad and toss well. Season to taste.
**3** Arrange the rocket leaves on a serving plate and top with the salad. Scatter the feta over the top and serve with crusty bread.

NUTRITION PER SERVE (6)
Protein 30 g; Fat 12 g; Carbohydrate 2.5 g; Dietary Fibre 3 g; Cholesterol 87 mg; 960 kJ (230 Cal)

### COOK'S FILE

**Note:** Buy semi-dried tomatoes at good supermarkets and delicatessens.

# STIR-FRIES AND PAN-FRIES

## CHICKEN STIR-FRY WITH SNOWPEA SPROUTS

Preparation time: 15 minutes
Total cooking time: 15 minutes
Serves 4

2 tablespoons oil
1 onion, finely sliced
3 makrut (kaffir) lime leaves, shredded
3 chicken breast fillets, cut into 2 cm ($3/4$ inch) cubes
1 red capsicum (pepper), sliced
60 ml ($1/4$ cup) lime juice
100 ml ($3^1/2$ fl oz) soy sauce
100 g ($3^1/2$ oz) snowpea (mangetout) sprouts
2 tablespoons chopped coriander (cilantro) leaves

**1** Heat a wok or frying pan over medium heat, add the oil and swirl to coat. Add the onion and lime leaves and stir-fry for 3–5 minutes, or until the onion begins to soften. Add the chicken and cook for a further 4 minutes. Add the capsicum and continue to cook for 2–3 minutes.
**2** Stir in the lime juice and soy sauce and cook for 1–2 minutes, or until the sauce reduces slightly. Add the sprouts and coriander. Cook until the sprouts have wilted. Serve with steamed rice and coriander and chilli, if desired.

NUTRITION PER SERVE
Protein 45 g; Fat 15 g; Carbohydrate 5.5 g; Dietary Fibre 2 g; Cholesterol 90 mg; 1375 kJ (330 Cal)

### COOK'S FILE

**Variation:** Use the chicken, soy sauce and lime juice as a base, and add or subtract ingredients to your taste.

## STIR-FRIED CHICKEN TORTILLAS

Preparation time: 10 minutes
Total cooking time: 15 minutes
Serves 4

2 tablespoons olive oil
1 onion, halved and
  thinly sliced
2 green capsicums (peppers),
  thinly sliced
3 chicken breast fillets, cut into
  2 cm (³⁄₄ inch) strips
35 g (1¼ oz) packet taco
  seasoning
200 g (7 oz) jar taco sauce
4 tortillas
160 g (²⁄₃ cup) sour cream

**1** Heat half the oil in a frying pan, add the onion and capsicum and cook for 5 minutes, or until soft. Remove from the pan and set aside.
**2** Add the remaining oil to the pan, add the chicken and cook, stirring, for 4–5 minutes. Add the taco seasoning and the onion and capsicum, stir to combine and cook for 1 minute. Then add the taco sauce and scrape up any bits from the bottom of the pan. Season.
**3** Heat the tortillas following the packet instructions. Place on individual plates and spoon the chicken onto one side of the tortillas. Spoon on the sour cream, roll up and serve.

**NUTRITION PER SERVE**
Protein 40 g; Fat 30 g; Carbohydrate 70 g; Dietary Fibre 5 g; Cholesterol 115 mg; 3075 kJ (735 Cal)

## CHICKEN ASPARAGUS STIR-FRY

Preparation time: 15 minutes
Total cooking time: 10 minutes
Serves 4

2 tablespoons oil
1 clove garlic, crushed
10 cm (4 inch) piece fresh ginger, peeled and thinly sliced
3 chicken breast fillets, sliced
4 spring onions (scallions), sliced
200 g (7 oz) fresh asparagus spears, sliced on the diagonal
2 tablespoons soy sauce
40 g ($1/3$ cup) slivered almonds, roasted

**1** Heat a wok or large frying pan over high heat, add the oil and swirl to coat. Add the garlic, ginger and chicken and stir-fry for 1–2 minutes, or until the chicken changes colour.
**2** Add the spring onion and asparagus and stir-fry for a further 2 minutes, or until the spring onion is soft.
**3** Stir in the soy sauce and 60 ml ($1/4$ cup) water, cover and simmer for 2 minutes, or until the chicken is tender and the vegetables are slightly crisp. Sprinkle with the almonds and serve over steamed rice or hokkien (egg) noodles.

**NUTRITION PER SERVE**
Protein 30 g; Fat 12 g; Carbohydrate 2 g; Dietary Fibre 1 g; Cholesterol 60 mg; 1010 kJ (240 Cal)

# CREAMY CHICKEN WITH TARRAGON

Preparation time: 5 minutes
Total cooking time: 20 minutes
Serves 4

5 chicken breast fillets, cut into 1 cm ($\frac{1}{2}$ inch) slices
2 tablespoons oil
1 tablespoon chopped French tarragon
250 ml (1 cup) cream
1 tablespoon lemon juice

**1** Lightly season the chicken with white pepper. Heat a wok or shallow frying pan over high heat, add the oil and swirl to coat. Add the chicken, in batches, and cook over medium heat for 3–4 minutes, or until browned. Return all the chicken to the pan and stir through the tarragon.

**2** Add the cream, bring to the boil and boil for 3 minutes, or until the sauce has thickened slightly. Add the lemon juice, season with salt and ground black pepper and serve with a green salad and buttered noodles.

**NUTRITION PER SERVE**
Protein 70 g; Fat 45 g; Carbohydrate 2 g; Dietary Fibre 0 g; Cholesterol 315 mg; 2800 kJ (670 Cal)

### COOK'S FILE

**Note:** If preparing in advance, add the lemon juice after reheating to serve. Avoid using Russian tarragon, which has a less subtle, slightly aniseed flavour. Tarragon vinegar is a good substitute for lemon juice.

## PARSLEY AND PARMESAN CRUMBED CHICKEN

Preparation time: 15 minutes + 30 minutes refrigeration
Total cooking time: 30 minutes
Serves 4

4 chicken breast fillets
plain (all-purpose) flour, for coating
75 g (3/4 cup) dry breadcrumbs
50 g (1/2 cup) freshly grated Parmesan cheese
15 g (1/2 cup) chopped flat-leaf (Italian) parsley
1 egg, lightly beaten
2 tablespoons milk
60 ml (1/4 cup) oil

**1** Flatten the chicken between 2 sheets of plastic wrap with a meat mallet or rolling pin. Coat in the flour.

**2** Combine the breadcrumbs, Parmesan and parsley. Combine the egg and milk in a separate bowl. Coat the fillets by dipping them first into the egg, and then into the crumb mixture. Press the crumb mixture onto the chicken and refrigerate for 30 minutes.

**3** Heat the oil in a frying pan over medium heat. Add two of the chicken breasts and cook, turning once, for 10–15 minutes, or until the chicken is cooked through. Set aside and repeat with the remaining chicken. Serve with lemon and boiled potatoes drizzled with butter and chives.

**NUTRITION PER SERVE**
Protein 35 g; Fat 23 g; Carbohydrate 17 g; Dietary Fibre 1 g; Cholesterol 118 mg; 1782 kJ (425 Cal)

### COOK'S FILE

**Note:** This dish can be prepared ahead and kept in the refrigerator overnight, or wrapped tightly and frozen.

## PEPPERED CHICKEN STIR-FRY

Preparation time: 10 minutes
Total cooking time: 10 minutes
Serves 4

1 tablespoon oil
2 chicken breast fillets, cut into strips
2½ teaspoons seasoned peppercorns (see Note)
1 onion, cut into wedges
1 red capsicum (pepper), cut into strips
2 tablespoons oyster sauce
1 teaspoon soy sauce
1 teaspoon sugar

**1** Heat a wok or frying pan over high heat, add the oil and swirl to coat. Add the chicken strips and stir-fry for 2–3 minutes, or until browned.
**2** Add the peppercorns and stir-fry until fragrant. Add the onion and capsicum and stir-fry for 2 minutes, or until the vegetables have softened slightly.
**3** Reduce the heat and stir in the oyster sauce, soy and sugar. Serve hot with steamed rice or Asian noodles.

**NUTRITION PER SERVE**
Protein 18 g; Fat 6.5 g; Carbohydrate 6 g; Dietary Fibre 1 g; Cholesterol 40 mg; 665 kJ (160 Cal)

**COOK'S FILE**

**Note:** Seasoned peppercorns are available in the herb and spice section of supermarkets.

1

2

3

## CHICKEN SAN CHOY BAU

Preparation time: 10 minutes
Total cooking time: 5 minutes
Serves 4

1 tablespoon oil
700 g (1 lb 9 oz) minced (ground) chicken
2 cloves garlic, finely chopped
100 g (3½ oz) can water chestnuts, drained, chopped
1½ tablespoons oyster sauce
3 teaspoons soy sauce
1 teaspoon sugar
5 spring onions (scallions), finely sliced
4 whole lettuce leaves

**1** Heat a wok or frying pan over high heat, add the oil and swirl to coat. Add the chicken mince and garlic and stir-fry for 3–4 minutes, or until browned and cooked through, breaking up any lumps with the back of a spoon. Pour off any excess liquid.

**2** Reduce the heat and add the water chestnuts, oyster sauce, soy sauce, sugar and spring onion.

**3** Trim the lettuce leaves around the edges to neaten them and to form a cup shape. Divide the chicken and vegetable mixture among the lettuce cups and serve hot, with extra oyster sauce, if desired.

**NUTRITION PER SERVE**
Protein 40 g; Fat 9 g; Carbohydrate 6 g; Dietary Fibre 2 g; Cholesterol 88 mg; 1142 kJ (273 Cal)

# SWEET CHILLI STIR-FRY

Preparation time: 10 minutes
Total cooking time: 10 minutes
Serves 4–6

375 g (13 oz) hokkien (egg) noodles
4 chicken thigh fillets, cut into small pieces (see Note)
1–2 tablespoons sweet chilli sauce
2 teaspoons fish sauce
1 tablespoon oil
100 g (3½ oz) baby sweet corn, halved lengthways
150 g (5½ oz) sugar snap peas, topped and tailed
1 tablespoon lime juice

**1** Place the noodles in a large bowl, cover with boiling water and gently break apart with a fork. Leave for 5 minutes, then drain.
**2** Combine the chicken, sweet chilli sauce and fish sauce in a bowl.
**3** Heat a wok or frying pan over high heat, add the oil and swirl to coat. Add the chicken pieces and stir-fry for 3–5 minutes, or until cooked through. Then add the corn and sugar snap peas and stir-fry for 2 minutes. Add the noodles and lime juice and serve.

NUTRITION PER SERVE (6)
Protein 30 g; Fat 6.5 g; Carbohydrate 50 g; Dietary Fibre 4 g; Cholesterol 53 mg; 1593 kJ (380 Cal)

### COOK'S FILE

**Note:** If thigh fillets are unavailable, use 3 breast fillets.

## TANGY ORANGE AND GINGER CHICKEN

Preparation time: 15 minutes
Total cooking time: 15–20 minutes
Serves 4

3 tablespoons light olive oil
10 chicken thigh fillets,
    cut into small pieces
3 teaspoons grated fresh ginger
1 teaspoon grated orange zest
125 ml (1/2 cup) chicken stock
2 teaspoons honey
550 g (1 lb 4 oz) bok choy (pak choi), trimmed and halved
toasted sesame seeds,
    to garnish

**1** Heat a wok or frying pan over high heat, add the oil and swirl to coat. Add the chicken, in batches, and stir-fry for 3–4 minutes, or until golden.
**2** Return all the chicken to the pan, add the ginger and orange zest, and cook for 20 seconds, or until fragrant. Add the stock and the honey and stir to combine. Increase the heat and cook for 3–4 minutes, or until the sauce has thickened slightly. Add the bok choy and cook until slightly wilted. Season with salt and freshly ground black pepper. Sprinkle with toasted sesame seeds and serve with boiled rice.

**NUTRITION PER SERVE**
Protein 70 g; Fat 20 g; Carbohydrate 3.5 g; Dietary Fibre 0.5 g; Cholesterol 150 mg; 2005 kJ (480 Cal)

## SMOKED CHICKEN AND SPINACH STIR-FRY

Preparation time: 10 minutes
Total cooking time: 10 minutes
Serves 4

300 g (10½ oz) smoked chicken breast (see Note)
1 tablespoon olive oil
100 g (3½ oz) marinated chargrilled (griddled) capsicum (pepper), cut into thin strips
50 g (⅓ cup) pine nuts
500 g (1 lb 2 oz) English spinach, trimmed
1 tablespoon light sour cream
2 teaspoons wholegrain mustard
3 tablespoons basil, shredded

**1** Cut the chicken into thin strips.
**2** Heat a wok or frying pan over high heat, add the oil and swirl to coat. Add the chicken, capsicum and pine nuts and stir-fry for 3–4 minutes, or until the nuts are golden. Add the spinach and stir-fry for 2–3 minutes, or until wilted.
**3** Stir through the sour cream, mustard and basil. Season and serve with noodles, if desired.

**NUTRITION PER SERVE**
Protein 22 g; Fat 13 g; Carbohydrate 2.5 g; Dietary Fibre 4.5 g; Cholesterol 45 mg; 900 kJ (215 Cal)

### COOK'S FILE

**Note:** Smoked chicken breast and marinated chargrilled capsicum are available at speciality delicatessens.

## CHICKEN MEATBALLS

Preparation time: 15 minutes
Total cooking time: 30 minutes
Serves 4–6

500 g (1 lb 2 oz) minced (ground) chicken
20 g (1/4 cup) fresh breadcrumbs
2 teaspoons finely chopped thyme
2 tablespoons oil
1 onion, finely chopped
2 x 425 g (15 oz) cans diced tomatoes
2 teaspoons balsamic vinegar
250 ml (1 cup) chicken stock

**1** Combine the chicken, breadcrumbs and thyme in a large bowl and season well. Roll a tablespoon of the mixture between your hands to make a meatball, and then repeat with the remaining mixture.
**2** Heat the oil in a large frying pan and fry the meatballs in batches for 5–8 minutes, or until golden brown. Remove from the pan and drain on paper towels.
**3** Add the onion to the pan and cook for 2–3 minutes, or until softened. Add the tomato, vinegar and stock, return the meatballs to the pan, then reduce the heat and simmer for 10 minutes, or until the sauce thickens and the meatballs are cooked through. Serve with pasta and garnish with basil and grated Parmesan cheese, if desired.

**NUTRITION PER SERVE (6)**
Protein 20 g; Fat 8.5 g; Carbohydrate 7.5 g; Dietary Fibre 2 g; Cholesterol 42 mg; 812 kJ (194 Cal)

## CHICKEN SAUSAGE STIR-FRY

Preparation time: 15 minutes
Total cooking time: 25 minutes
Serves 4–6

6 thick chicken sausages
2 tablespoons chicken stock
1 tablespoon oyster sauce
1 teaspoon soy sauce
1 tablespoon oil
1 red onion, halved, thinly sliced
1 red capsicum (pepper), julienned
100 g (3½ oz) snowpeas (mangetout), halved if large

**1** Place the sausages on a griller (broiler) tray and cook under high heat, turning, for 10–15 minutes, or until cooked through. Allow to cool and thinly slice on the diagonal.
**2** Combine the chicken stock, oyster sauce and soy sauce in a bowl.
**3** Heat a wok or frying pan over high heat, add the oil and swirl to coat. Add the onion and stir-fry for 2 minutes, then add the capsicum, snowpeas and sausage and stir-fry for 1–2 minutes. Add the chicken stock mixture and stir-fry for a further 3–5 minutes, or until the vegetables are cooked and the sauce has reduced slightly. Season with salt and pepper and serve with hokkien (egg) noodles.

NUTRITION PER SERVE (6)
Protein 15 g; Fat 26 g; Carbohydrate 6 g; Dietary Fibre 4 g; Cholesterol 57 mg; 1305 kJ (312 Cal)

## MIDDLE-EASTERN STIR-FRY

Preparation time: 10 minutes
Total cooking time: 20 minutes
Serves 4

2 tablespoons oil
2 chicken breast fillets, thinly sliced
1 red onion, thinly sliced
310 g (11 oz) can chickpeas, drained
75 g ($^1/_2$ cup) unsalted pistachio kernels
1 tomato, chopped
juice of 1 orange
7 g ($^1/_4$ cup) finely chopped flat-leaf (Italian) parsley

**1** Heat a wok or frying pan over high heat, add half the oil and swirl to coat. Stir-fry the chicken, in batches, for 3–5 minutes, or until cooked. Remove from the pan and keep warm.
**2** Add the remaining oil to the wok and stir-fry the onion for 2 minutes, then add the chickpeas, pistachio kernels and tomato, and stir-fry for 3–5 minutes, or until the chickpeas are warmed through.
**3** Pour in the orange juice, return the chicken and its juices to the wok and stir-fry until half the juice has evaporated. Stir through the parsley. Season with salt and ground black pepper and serve with couscous.

**NUTRITION PER SERVE**
Protein 37 g; Fat 25 g; Carbohydrate 17 g; Dietary Fibre 6.5 g; Cholesterol 60 mg; 1785 kJ (425 Cal)

1

2

3

# BARBECUES AND GRILLS

## SESAME CHICKEN KEBABS

Preparation time: 10 minutes +
30 minutes soaking +
2 hours marinating
Total cooking time: 10 minutes
Serves 4

60 ml (¼ cup) oil
2 tablespoons soy sauce
2 tablespoons honey
1 tablespoon grated fresh ginger
1 tablespoon sesame oil
4 large chicken breast fillets, cut into 2 cm (¾ inch) cubes
8 spring onions (scallions, cut into 2 cm (¾ inch) lengths
1 tablespoon toasted sesame seeds

**1** Soak 12 wooden skewers in water for 30 minutes to prevent burning. To make the marinade, whisk together the oil, soy sauce, honey, ginger and sesame oil. Thread the chicken and spring onion alternately onto the skewers and place in a glass dish. Pour the marinade over the skewers, cover and refrigerate for 2 hours, or overnight if time permits.
**2** Place the skewers on a griller (broiler) tray and place under a hot griller (broiler). Baste with the marinade and cook, turning once, for 10 minutes, or until cooked through. Sprinkle with the sesame seeds. Serve with chargrilled vegetables, if desired.

**NUTRITION PER SERVE**
Protein 55 g; Fat 25 g; Carbohydrate 13 g; Dietary Fibre 1 g; Cholesterol 120 mg; 2180 kJ (520 cal)

### COOK'S FILE

**Note:** These kebabs can also be barbecued.
**Hint:** To toast sesame seeds, place in a dry pan and shake over moderate heat until the seeds are golden.

1

2

## DRUMSTICKS IN TOMATO AND MANGO CHUTNEY

Preparation time: 10 minutes + 2 hours marinating
Total cooking time: 45 minutes
Serves 4

8 chicken drumsticks, scored
1 tablespoon mustard powder
2 tablespoons tomato sauce
1 tablespoon sweet mango chutney
1 teaspoon Worcestershire sauce
1 tablespoon Dijon mustard
30 g (¼ cup) raisins
1 tablespoon oil

**1** Preheat the oven to 200°C (400°F/Gas 6). Toss the chicken in the mustard powder and season.
**2** Combine the tomato sauce, chutney, Worcestershire sauce, mustard, raisins and oil. Spoon over the chicken and toss well to coat evenly. Marinate for 2 hours, or overnight if time permits, turning halfway through.
**3** Put the chicken in a shallow baking tray and bake for 45 minutes, or until the flesh pulls away from the bone.

NUTRITION PER SERVE
Protein 25 g; Fat 15 g; Carbohydrate 3.5 g; Dietary Fibre 0.5 g; Cholesterol 103 mg; 1005 kJ (240 Cal)

### COOK'S FILE

**Serving suggestion:** Serve with toasted Turkish bread and a mixture of yoghurt, cucumber and mint.

# CHARGRILLED CHICKEN SALAD WITH ROCKET AND CANNELLINI BEANS

Preparation time: 10 minutes
Total cooking time: 20 minutes
Serves 4

80 ml (1/3 cup) lemon juice
3 cloves garlic, crushed
15 g (1/4 cup) basil, finely chopped
1 teaspoon soft brown sugar
125 ml (1/2 cup) olive oil
4 chicken breast fillets
400 g (14 oz) can cannellini beans, rinsed and drained
100 g (3 1/2 oz) small rocket (arugula) leaves

**1** Prepare the vinaigrette by whisking together the lemon juice, garlic, basil, sugar and olive oil. Season.
**2** Pour a third of the dressing over the chicken breasts to coat. Chargrill (griddle) or barbecue the chicken, in batches, over medium heat for 10 minutes, turning once, or until cooked through.
**3** Meanwhile, combine the beans and rocket with the remaining vinaigrette, toss well and season. Slice the chicken across the grain into 1.5 cm (5/8 inch) pieces. Serve the rocket and beans topped with the sliced chicken.

**NUTRITION PER SERVE**
Protein 35 g; Fat 35 g; Carbohydrate 13 g; Dietary Fibre 7.5 g; Cholesterol 60 mg; 2045 kJ (490 Cal)

1

2

## CHICKEN WINGS MARINATED IN SOY

Preparation time: 10 minutes +
    20 minutes refrigeration
Total cooking time: 50 minutes
Serves 4

125 ml (½ cup) soy sauce
3 tablespoons honey
2 cloves garlic, crushed
60 ml (¼ cup) sweet chilli sauce
80 ml (⅓ cup) lemon juice
10 g (½ cup) lightly packed
    mint, roughly chopped
16 chicken wings

**1** Preheat the oven to 200°C (400°F/ Gas 6). Mix together the soy, honey, garlic, sweet chilli sauce, lemon juice and mint. Put the chicken wings in a flat dish, pour on the marinade, cover with plastic wrap and refrigerate for 20 minutes.

**2** Place the wings and any excess marinade into a baking dish and bake for 50 minutes, or until the wings are cooked through and caramelized. Turn the wings once or twice during cooking to ensure even caramelization.

**NUTRITION PER SERVE**
Protein 25 g; Fat 7 g; Carbohydrate 18 g; Dietary Fibre 0 g; Cholesterol 105 mg; 1004 kJ (240 Cal)

### COOK'S FILE

**Note:** The wings can be eaten by themselves or, for a more substantial meal, serve with steamed rice and a green salad. They can marinate overnight and be cooked the next day.

1

2

## CHICKEN WITH YOGHURT SAUCE

Preparation time: 10 minutes
Total cooking time: 20 minutes
Serves 4

3 tablespoons olive oil
2 teaspoons curry powder
4 chicken breast fillets
90 g ($1/3$ cup) Greek-style plain yoghurt
1 tablespoon lemon juice
1 clove garlic, crushed
$1^{1}/_{2}$ tablespoons chopped mint

**1** Combine 2 tablespoons of the oil and the curry powder in a bowl, add the chicken and toss to coat. Season with salt and ground black pepper.
**2** To make the sauce, combine the yoghurt, lemon juice, garlic and mint in a bowl. Season, then refrigerate until ready to serve.
**3** Heat the remaining oil in a frying pan over medium heat and cook the chicken, in batches, for 5 minutes each side, or until cooked through. Slice into thirds and serve with a dollop of the yoghurt sauce and salad, if desired.

**NUTRITION PER SERVE**
Protein 30 g; Fat 18 g; Carbohydrate 2 g; Dietary Fibre 0.5 g; Cholesterol 65 mg; 1205 kJ (285 Cal)

1

2

3

## PERSIAN CHICKEN SKEWERS

Preparation time: 10 minutes +
30 minutes soaking +
overnight marinating
Total cooking time: 10 minutes
Serves 4

2 teaspoons ground cardamom
1/2 teaspoon ground turmeric
1 teaspoon ground allspice
4 cloves garlic, crushed
60 ml (1/4 cup) lemon juice
3 tablespoons olive oil
4 large chicken thigh fillets, excess fat removed, cut into 3–4 cm (1 1/4–1 1/2 inch) cubes

**1** Soak 8 wooden skewers in water for 30 minutes to prevent them burning. To make the marinade, whisk together the spices, garlic, lemon juice and oil. Season with salt and freshly ground black pepper.
**2** Toss the chicken in the spice mixture. Thread the chicken onto skewers and place on a tray. Cover and refrigerate overnight.
**3** Place the skewers on a griller (broiler) tray and cook under a hot grill (broiler), or place in a chargrill pan (griddle) for 4 minutes each side, or until cooked through. Serve with a green salad, lemon wedges and plain yoghurt, if desired.

**NUTRITION PER SERVE**
Protein 35 g; Fat 18 g; Carbohydrate 0.5 g; Dietary Fibre 0.5 g; Cholesterol 75 mg; 1259 kJ (300 Cal)

## TANDOORI CHICKEN

Preparation time: 10 minutes +
  1 hour marinating
Total cooking time: 30 minutes
Serves 4

125 g (½ cup) Greek-style
  plain yoghurt
2 tablespoons tandoori paste
2 cloves garlic, crushed
2 tablespoons lime juice
1½ teaspoons garam masala
2 tablespoons finely chopped
  coriander (cilantro) leaves
6 chicken thigh fillets,
  excess fat removed

**1** Combine the yoghurt, tandoori paste, garlic, lime juice, garam masala and coriander in a bowl and mix well.
**2** Add the chicken, coat well, cover and refrigerate for at least 1 hour, or overnight if time permits.
**3** Preheat a barbecue or chargrill (griddle) pan and lightly brush with oil. Cook the chicken, in batches if necessary, for 10–15 minutes on medium heat, turning the chicken once and basting with the remaining marinade, until golden and cooked through. Serve with cucumber raita and naan bread.

**NUTRITION PER SERVE**
Protein 27 g; Fat 3.5 g; Carbohydrate 2 g; Dietary Fibre 0 g; Cholesterol 60 mg; 635 kJ (150 Cal)

1

2

3

## CHICKEN TIKKA KEBABS

Preparation time: 10 minutes +
  30 minutes soaking +
  2 hours marinating
Total cooking time: 10 minutes
Serves 4

10 chicken thigh fillets, cubed
1 red onion, cut into wedges
60 ml (1/4 cup) tikka paste
125 ml (1/2 cup) coconut milk
2 tablespoons lemon juice

**1** Soak 8 skewers in water for 30 minutes to prevent burning. Thread 2 pieces of chicken and a wedge of onion alternately along each skewer.

**2** Combine the tikka paste, coconut milk and lemon juice in a jar with a lid. Season and shake well to combine. Pour the mixture over the skewers and marinate for at least 2 hours.

**3** Place the skewers on a griller (broiler) tray under a hot griller (broiler) and cook, basting, for 7–8 minutes, or until the chicken is cooked through. Serve with brown rice and a crisp green salad.

### NUTRITION PER SERVE
Protein 50 g; Fat 13 g; Carbohydrate 4 g; Dietary Fibre 1.5 g; Cholesterol 114 mg; 1457 kJ (350 Cal)

### COOK'S FILE

**Note:** Any leftover marinade can be heated to boiling and used as a sauce.

## MARINATED PESTO CHICKEN

Preparation time: 15 minutes +
1 hour marinating
Total cooking time: 10 minutes
Serves 4

100 g (2 cups) firmly packed basil
4 cloves garlic
50 g (1/2 cup) freshly grated Parmesan cheese
50 g (1/3 cup) pine nuts, toasted
80 ml (1/3 cup) lemon juice
250 ml (1 cup) olive oil
4 chicken breast fillets

**1** Place the basil, garlic, Parmesan, pine nuts and lemon juice in a food processor and process until combined. Gradually add the oil, with the motor running, and process until smooth.

**2** Reserve 185 ml (3/4 cup) of the pesto. Coat the chicken with the remaining pesto and marinate for at least 1 hour, or overnight if time permits.

**3** Place the chicken on a tray and cook under a medium griller (broiler) for 5 minutes on each side, or until cooked, brushing with any remaining marinade during cooking. Serve with roasted vegetables and the reserved pesto.

**NUTRITION PER SERVE**
Protein 30 g; Fat 75 g; Carbohydrate 1.5 g; Dietary Fibre 1 g; Cholesterol 65 mg; 3338 kJ (797 Cal)

# MARINADES AND GLAZES

### LIME AND GINGER GLAZE

In a small pan combine 160 g ($1/2$ cup) lime marmalade, 60 ml ($1/4$ cup) lime juice, 2 tablespoons sherry, 2 tablespoons soft brown sugar and 2 teaspoons finely grated ginger. Stir over low heat until it reaches a liquid consistency. Pour over 1 kg (2 lb 4 oz) chicken wings and toss well to combine. Cover and refrigerate for 2 hours or overnight. Cook in a 190°C (375°F/Gas 5) oven for 40 minutes, or until cooked through. Makes 250 ml (1 cup).

### HONEY SOY MARINADE

Combine 90 g ($1/4$ cup) honey, 60 ml ($1/4$ cup) soy sauce, 1 crushed garlic clove, 2 tablespoons sake and $1/2$ teaspoon Chinese five-spice powder. Remove excess fat from 500 g (1 lb 2 oz) chicken thigh fillets. Pour on the marinade and toss well to combine. Cover and refrigerate for 2 hours or overnight. Cook on a hot barbecue for 10 minutes, turning once, or until cooked through. Makes 170 ml ($2/3$ cup).

### REDCURRANT GLAZE

In a small saucepan combine a 340 g (12 oz) jar redcurrant jelly, 2 tablespoons lemon juice, 2 tablespoons brandy and 1 teaspoon chopped thyme, and stir over low heat until it reaches a liquid consistency. Pour the marinade over 500 g (1 lb 2 oz) chicken breast fillets and toss well to combine. Cover and refrigerate for 2 hours or overnight. Cook in a 190°C (375°F/Gas 5) oven for 20 minutes, or until cooked through. Makes 250 ml (1 cup).

### TANDOORI MARINADE

Soak 8 wooden skewers in water for 30 minutes to prevent burning. Combine 2 tablespoons tandoori paste, 250 g (1 cup) plain yoghurt and 1 tablespoon lime juice. Cut 500 g (1 lb 2 oz) chicken tenderloins in half lengthways and thread onto skewers. Pour on the marinade and toss well to combine. Cover and refrigerate for 1–2 hours. Place under a hot griller (broiler) and cook, basting with the marinade, until cooked through. Makes 315 ml ($1^{1}/4$ cups).

### MEXICAN MARINADE

Combine 440 g (1 lb) bottled taco sauce, 2 tablespoons lime juice and 2 tablespoons chopped coriander (cilantro) leaves. Pour the marinade over 1 kg (2 lb 4 oz) scored chicken drumsticks and toss well to combine. Cover and refrigerate for 2 hours or overnight. Cook in a 190°C (375°F/Gas 5) oven for 30 minutes, or until cooked through. Makes 315 ml ($1^{1}/4$ cups).

### THAI MARINADE

Combine 2 tablespoons fish sauce, 2 tablespoons lime juice, 1 crushed garlic clove, 1 finely chopped stalk lemon grass, 2 teaspoons soft brown sugar, 125 g ($1/2$ cup) coconut cream and 2 tablespoons chopped coriander (cilantro) leaves. Pour the marinade over 1 kg (2 lb 4 oz) chicken drumsticks and toss well to combine. Cover and refrigerate for 2 hours or overnight. Cook in a 190°C (375°F/Gas 5) oven for 30 minutes, or until cooked through. Makes 185 ml ($3/4$ cup).

*Clockwise from top left: Lime and ginger glaze; Tandoori marinade; Mexican marinade; Thai marinade; Redcurrant glaze; Honey soy marinade.*

## CHERMOULA CHICKEN

Preparation time: 10 minutes +
  2 hours marinating
Total cooking time: 15 minutes
Serves 4

10 g (½ cup) flat-leaf (Italian) parsley
7 g (¼ cup) coriander (cilantro) leaves
2 cloves garlic, roughly chopped
60 ml (¼ cup) lemon juice
3 teaspoons ground cumin
1 tablespoon chopped preserved lemon
125 ml (½ cup) olive oil
4 chicken breast fillets, flattened

**1** To make the marinade, combine the parsley, coriander, garlic, lemon juice, cumin and preserved lemon in a food processor or blender and process until well combined. While the motor is running, gradually add the oil in a thin stream until smooth. Season.
**2** Place the chicken in a large, flat dish and pour over the marinade. Marinate for 2 hours, or overnight if time permits.
**3** Grease four sheets of foil and place a chicken breast in the centre of each. Spoon any extra marinade over the chicken. Fold over the foil and secure the ends. Place the parcels under a hot griller (broiler) and cook for 10–12 minutes without turning, or until cooked through. Remove from the foil parcels, cut into slices and serve with couscous.

**NUTRITION PER SERVE**
Protein 25 g; Fat 33 g; Carbohydrate 0.5 g; Dietary Fibre 0.5 g; Cholesterol 60 mg; 1690 kJ (405 Cal)

### COOK'S FILE

**Note:** To flatten chicken breast fillets, put them between two pieces of plastic wrap and hit with a meat mallet or the palm of your hand.

# BLACKENED CAJUN SPICED CHICKEN

Preparation time: 15 minutes +
 30 minutes standing
Total cooking time: 1 hour
Serves 4

1 1/2 tablespoons onion powder
1 1/2 tablespoons garlic powder
2 teaspoons paprika
1 teaspoon white pepper
2 teaspoons dried thyme
1/2–1 teaspoon chilli powder
8 chicken drumsticks, scored

**1** Combine the herbs, spices and 1 teaspoon salt in a freezer bag. Place the drumsticks in the bag and shake until all the pieces are coated. Refrigerate the chicken for at least 30 minutes to allow the flavours to develop, or overnight if time permits.

**2** Cook the drumsticks on a barbecue or in a chargrill (griddle) pan for 55–60 minutes, or until slightly blackened and cooked through. Brush lightly with some oil to prevent drying out during cooking. Serve hot with salad and crusty bread.

**NUTRITION PER SERVE**
Protein 25 g; Fat 7 g; Carbohydrate 0 g; Dietary Fibre 0 g; Cholesterol 103 mg; 660 kJ (160 Cal)

### COOK'S FILE

**Note:** Chilli powder is very hot, so only use 1/2 teaspoon if a milder dish is desired.

## GRILLED CHICKEN SKEWERS

Preparation time: 20 minutes +
  2 hours marinating
Total cooking time: 10 minutes
Makes 8 skewers

32 chicken tenderloins
24 cherry tomatoes
6 cap mushrooms,
  cut into quarters
2 cloves garlic, crushed
zest of 1 lemon, grated
2 tablespoons lemon juice
2 tablespoons olive oil
1 tablespoon oregano leaves,
  chopped

**1** Soak 8 wooden skewers for at least 30 minutes to prevent burning. Thread a piece of chicken onto each skewer, followed by a tomato, then a piece of mushroom. Repeat three times for each skewer.
**2** Combine the garlic, lemon zest, lemon juice, olive oil and chopped oregano, pour over the skewers and toss well. Marinate for 2 hours, or overnight if time permits.
**3** Place the skewers on a barbecue plate and cook over high heat for 5 minutes each side, basting while cooking, or until the chicken is cooked and the tomatoes have shrivelled slightly. Serve hot with a green salad.

NUTRITION PER SKEWER
Protein 34 g; Fat 8 g; Carbohydrate 1 g; Dietary Fibre 1 g; Cholesterol 75 mg; 909 kJ (217 Cal)

### COOK'S FILE

**Note:** The skewers can be made in advance and marinated for a longer time and cooked when you are ready to eat them. They are delicious with a crispy green salad and potato wedges.

1

2

3

## ASIAN BARBECUED CHICKEN

Preparation time: 10 minutes + 2 hours marinating
Total cooking time: 25 minutes
Serves 4–6

2 cloves garlic, finely chopped
60 ml (1/4 cup) hoisin sauce
3 teaspoons light soy sauce
3 teaspoons honey
2 tablespoons tomato sauce or sweet chilli sauce
1 teaspoon sesame oil
2 spring onions (scallions), finely sliced
1.5 kg (3 lb 5 oz) chicken wings

**1** To make the marinade, combine the garlic, hoisin sauce, soy, honey, tomato sauce, sesame oil and spring onion in a small bowl.
**2** Pour over the chicken wings, cover and marinate in the refrigerator for 2 hours, or overnight if time permits.
**3** Place the chicken on a barbecue and cook, in batches, turning once, for 20–25 minutes, or until cooked and golden brown. Baste with the marinade during cooking. Heat any remaining marinade in a pan until boiling and serve as a sauce. Serve with a green salad.

NUTRITION PER SERVE (6)
Protein 26 g; Fat 8.5 g; Carbohydrate 9 g; Dietary Fibre 1.5 g; Cholesterol 111 mg; 916 kJ (219 Cal)

### COOK'S FILE

**Note:** The chicken can also be baked in a 180°C (350°F/Gas 4) oven for 30 minutes, and turned halfway through cooking.
**Variation:** Other cuts of chicken, such as drumsticks or breast or thigh fillets could be substituted, if desired.

1

2

3

## THAI DRUMSTICKS

Preparation time: 10 minutes +
  2 hours marinating
Total cooking time: 1 hour
Serves 6

3 tablespoons red curry paste
250 ml (1 cup) coconut milk
2 tablespoons lime juice
4 tablespoons finely chopped
  coriander (cilantro) leaves
12 chicken drumsticks, scored
1 kg (2 lb 4 oz) baby bok choy
  (pak choi)
2 tablespoons soy sauce
1 tablespoon oil

**1** Combine the curry paste, coconut milk, lime juice and coriander in a bowl. Place the chicken in a flat dish and pour on the marinade. Cover and marinate in the refrigerator for 2 hours, or overnight if time permits.
**2** Cook the chicken drumsticks on a barbecue for 50–60 minutes, or until cooked through.
**3** Trim the bok choy and combine with the soy sauce and oil, then cook on the barbecue or in a wok for 3–4 minutes, or until just wilted. Serve the chicken on a bed of bok choy.

**NUTRITION PER SERVE**
Protein 30 g; Fat 20 g; Carbohydrate 3 g; Dietary Fibre 5 g; Cholesterol 105 mg; 1250 kJ (300 Cal)

## PIRRI-PIRRI CHICKEN

Preparation time: 5 minutes + 1 hour marinating
Total cooking time: 1 hour
Serves 4

6 birdseye chillies, finely chopped, with seeds
1 teaspoon coarse salt
125 ml (½ cup) olive oil
185 ml (¾ cup) cider vinegar
1 clove garlic, crushed
4 chicken Maryland (leg quarter) pieces
4 lemon wedges

**1** Combine the chilli, salt, olive oil, vinegar and garlic in a jar. Seal and shake well to combine.
**2** Place the chicken pieces in a shallow dish and pour on the marinade. Cover and marinate for 1 hour, or overnight if time permits.
**3** Cook the chicken on a hot barbecue or chargrill pan (griddle), as close to the flame as possible, basting regularly with the marinade, for 50–60 minutes, or until the chicken is cooked through and the skin begins to crisp. Serve with lemon wedges, corn cobs and steamed green beans.

**NUTRITION PER SERVE**
Protein 27 g; Fat 30 g; Carbohydrate 0.5 g; Dietary Fibre 0.5 g; Cholesterol 60 mg; 1705 kJ (405 Cal)

### COOK'S FILE

**Note:** Any chicken cut that is still on the bone can be used in this recipe. Pirri-pirri is also excellent for barbecuing prawns (shrimp). Seed the chillies for a milder tasting dish.

# EVERYDAY FAMILY MEALS

## CHICKEN PROVENCALE

Preparation time: 15 minutes
Total cooking time: 1 hour 20 minutes
Serves 4–6

1 tablespoon olive oil
1.5 kg (3 lb 5 oz) chicken pieces
1 onion, chopped
1 red capsicum (pepper), chopped
80 ml (1/3 cup) white wine
80 ml (1/3 cup) chicken stock
425 g (15 oz) can chopped tomatoes
2 tablespoons tomato paste (purée)
90 g (1/2 cup) black olives
4 tablespoons shredded basil

**1** Heat the oil in a saucepan over high heat, add the chicken, in batches, and cook for 3–4 minutes, or until browned. Return all the chicken to the pan and add the onion and capsicum. Cook for 2–3 minutes, or until the onion is soft.
**2** Add the wine, stock, tomatoes, tomato paste and olives, and bring to the boil. Reduce the heat, cover and simmer for 30 minutes. Remove the lid, turn the chicken pieces over and cook for another 30 minutes, or until the chicken is tender and the cooking liquid has thickened. Season to taste with salt, black pepper and a little sugar, if desired. Sprinkle with the basil and serve with boiled rice.

**NUTRITION PER SERVE (6)**
Protein 35 g; Fat 10 g; Carbohydrate 5 g; Dietary Fibre 2 g; Cholesterol 115 mg; 1133 kJ (270 Cal)

## WHOLE CHICKEN WITH TARRAGON BUTTER

Preparation time: 15 minutes
Total cooking time: 1 hour 15 minutes
Serves 4

2 cloves garlic
200 g (7 oz) butter, softened
1 tablespoon tarragon, chopped (reserve the stalks)
1 tablespoon flat-leaf (Italian) parsley, finely chopped
1.8 kg (4 lb) corn-fed chicken
1 head garlic, cut through the centre

**1** Preheat the oven to 200°C (400°F/Gas 6). Crush the garlic and mix with the butter, tarragon and parsley, and season well.

**2** Loosen the skin of the chicken from the breast to the thigh with your fingers, taking care to not put any holes in the skin. Spread the tarragon butter under the loosened skin, using your fingers to spread the butter evenly. Stuff the cavity with 1/2 head of garlic and tarragon stalks. Tie the legs together with string to help keep the chicken's shape.

**3** Place the chicken in a baking dish and bake for 1 hour 15 minutes, or until cooked through. Serve with roasted vegetables.

**NUTRITION PER SERVE**
Protein 65 g; Fat 50 g; Carbohydrate 0.6 g; Dietary Fibre 0.6 g; Cholesterol 335 mg; 3054 kJ (730 Cal)

## CHICKEN AND ARTICHOKE PIZZA

Preparation time: 15 minutes
Total cooking time: 25 minutes
Serves 4

2 tablespoons extra virgin olive oil
170 g (6 oz) jar marinated artichokes, drained, quartered and juice reserved
2 large chicken thigh fillets, cut into bite-sized pieces
1 ready-made tomato pizza base (26 cm/10½ inch diameter)
1 small red onion, finely sliced
½ red capsicum (pepper), sliced
12 Kalamata olives
200 g (7 oz) bocconcini cheese, sliced

**1** Preheat the oven to 220°C (425°F/Gas 7). Heat the oil in a frying pan, add 2 tablespoons reserved artichoke juice and the chicken and cook over high heat for 3–4 minutes, or until the chicken is cooked through.
**2** Place the pizza base on an oven tray and scatter the chicken evenly over the base, reserving the oil from cooking. Scatter the artichokes, onion, capsicum and olives over the chicken, season with salt and black pepper, and add the bocconcini slices. Spoon the oil from cooking over the topping.
**3** Bake on the top shelf of the oven for 15–20 minutes, or until the topping begins to brown. Cut into wedges and serve.

**NUTRITION PER SERVE**
Protein 35 g; Fat 40 g; Carbohydrate 17 g; Dietary Fibre 2.5 g; Cholesterol 88 mg; 2309 kJ (550 Cal)

### COOK'S FILE

**Variation:** For a more cheesy base, sprinkle with grated mozzarella before assembling the pizza topping.

## BRAISED CHICKEN IN WHITE WINE WITH CAPSICUM AND ROSEMARY

Preparation time: 15 minutes
Total cooking time: 45 minutes
Serves 4

8 (1.2 kg/2 lb 11 oz) chicken pieces
2 red capsicums (peppers), cut into 2 cm (³/₄ inch) cubes
1 green capsicum (pepper), cut into 2 cm (³/₄ inch) cubes
1 red onion, cut into large chunks
3 rosemary sprigs
100 g (3½ oz) black olives
250 ml (1 cup) white wine
200 ml (7 fl oz) olive oil

**1** Preheat the oven to 200°C (400°F/Gas 6). Score the larger chicken pieces and combine in a large baking dish with the capsicum, onion, rosemary and olives. Season.
**2** Pour the wine and oil over the chicken and vegetables and bake for 45 minutes, or until the chicken is cooked. Baste the chicken during cooking with the juices.
**3** Remove from the oven and stand for 5 minutes. Skim excess oil from the top and serve.

NUTRITION PER SERVE
Protein 55 g; Fat 57 g; Carbohydrate 10 g; Dietary Fibre 4 g; Cholesterol 138 mg; 3237 kJ (773 Cal)

### COOK'S FILE

**Variation:** Any type of vegetables may be used instead of capsicum, for example, zucchini (courgette).

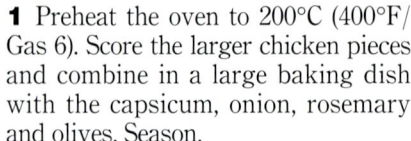

## CHICKEN CACCIATORE WITH FETA AND BLACK OLIVES

Preparation time: 15 minutes
Total cooking time: 1 hour
Serves 4

2 tablespoons oil
8 (1.2 kg/2 lb 11 oz) chicken pieces (with skin on)
1 onion, chopped
25 g (1 oz) oregano, leaves picked
2 tablespoons tomato paste (purée)
2 x 425 g (15 oz) cans crushed tomatoes
150 g (5½ oz) black olives
150 g (5½ oz) feta cheese, crumbled

**1** Heat half the oil in a saucepan and cook the chicken pieces, in batches, for 3–4 minutes, or until golden. Remove from the pan and set aside.
**2** In the same saucepan, heat the remaining oil and cook the onion and half the oregano leaves for 3 minutes, or until the onion is soft. Add the tomato paste and stir for 2 minutes, then add the tomato and chicken pieces.
**3** Simmer, covered, for 40–50 minutes, or until the chicken is cooked through. Add the olives and remaining oregano leaves. To serve, spoon into bowls and top with the crumbled feta.

**NUTRITION PER SERVE**
Protein 50 g; Fat 28 g; Carbohydrate 11 g; Dietary Fibre 5 g; Cholesterol 165 mg; 2110 kJ (505 Cal)

### COOK'S FILE

**Serving suggestion:** This dish is delicious served with fettucine.

## CHICKEN AND PASTA BAKE

Preparation time: 15 minutes
Total cooking time: 45 minutes
Serves 4

200 g (7 oz) spiral pasta
425 g (15 oz) can cream of mushroom or broccoli soup
250 g (1 cup) sour cream
1 teaspoon curry powder
1 barbecue chicken
250 g (9 oz) broccoli, cut into small pieces
80 g (1 cup) fresh breadcrumbs
185 g (1½ cups) grated Cheddar cheese

**1** Preheat the oven to 180°C (350°F/Gas 4). Bring a saucepan of salted water to the boil, add the pasta and cook for 10–12 minutes, or until *al dente*. Drain.
**2** Combine the soup, sour cream and curry powder and season to taste with freshly ground black pepper.
**3** Remove the meat from the chicken carcass and roughly chop. Combine the chicken with the pasta, broccoli and soup mixture. Spoon into four lightly greased 500 ml (2 cup) ovenproof dishes and sprinkle with the combined breadcrumbs and cheese. Bake for 25–30 minutes, or until the cheese melts.

**NUTRITION PER SERVE**
Protein 67 g; Fat 47 g; Carbohydrate 54.5 g; Dietary Fibre 7.5 g; Cholesterol 254 mg; 3812 kJ (911 Cal)

### COOK'S FILE

**Variation:** This recipe can be made in a 2 litre (8 cup) ovenproof dish and baked for 40 minutes.

1

2

## BAKED CHICKEN AND LEEK RISOTTO

Preparation time: 10 minutes
Total cooking time: 40 minutes
Serves 4–6

60 g (2¼ oz) butter
1 leek, thinly sliced
2 chicken breast fillets, cut into 2 cm (¾ inch) cubes
440 g (2 cups) arborio rice (see Note)
60 ml (¼ cup) white wine
1.25 litres (5 cups) chicken stock
35 g (⅓ cup) freshly grated Parmesan cheese
2 tablespoons thyme leaves
thyme leaves, to garnish
freshly grated Parmesan cheese, extra

**1** Preheat the oven to 150°C (300°F/Gas 2) and place a 5 litre (20 cup) ovenproof dish with a lid in the oven to warm. Heat the butter in a saucepan over medium heat, add the leek and cook for 2 minutes, or until soft.
**2** Add the chicken and cook, stirring, for 2–3 minutes, or until it colours. Add the rice and stir so that it is well coated with butter. Cook for 1 minute.
**3** Add the wine and stock and bring to the boil. Pour the mixture into the warm ovenproof dish and cover. Place in the oven and cook for 30 minutes, stirring halfway through. Remove from the oven and stir through the Parmesan and thyme leaves. Season to taste. Sprinkle with extra thyme leaves and extra Parmesan and serve.

**NUTRITION PER SERVE (6)**
Protein 28 g; Fat 15 g; Carbohydrate 60 g; Dietary Fibre 3 g; Cholesterol 75 mg; 2014 kJ (480 Cal)

### COOK'S FILE

**Note:** Arborio rice is a special short-grain rice for making risotto.

## QUICK SHORT CHICKEN RECIPES

### CHICKEN, LEEK AND SWEET POTATO ONE POT

Preparation time: 15 minutes
Total cooking time: 1 hour 40 minutes
Serves 4

2 tablespoons olive oil
1.5 kg (3 lb 5 oz) chicken pieces, on the bone
1 leek, cut into 2 cm (3/4 inch) slices
2 cloves garlic, crushed
2 tablespoons plain (all-purpose) flour
500 ml (2 cups) chicken stock
600 g (1 lb 5 oz) orange sweet potato, peeled and cut into chunks
2 tablespoons thyme

**1** Preheat the oven to 220°C (425°F/Gas 7). Heat 1 tablespoon of the oil in a large ovenproof casserole dish, add the chicken, in batches, and cook for 3–4 minutes, or until browned. Set aside. Add the remaining oil and cook the leek and garlic for 2 minutes, or until soft.

**2** Add the flour to the dish and cook, stirring, for about 1 minute to brown the flour. Gradually add the stock, stirring until the sauce boils and thickens. Remove from the heat. Return the chicken to the pan.

**3** Add the sweet potato and half the thyme. Cover the casserole and bake for 1 1/2 hours, or until the chicken is cooked and the sweet potato is tender. Season and scatter with the remaining thyme. Serve with steamed rice.

**NUTRITION PER SERVE**
Protein 80 g; Fat 25 g; Carbohydrate 25 g; Dietary Fibre 4 g; Cholesterol 260 mg; 2778 kJ (665 Cal)

## CHICKEN, MUSHROOM AND BROWN LENTIL CASSEROLE

Preparation time: 10 minutes
Total cooking time: 1 hour
Serves 4

50 g (1¾ oz) butter
180 g (6 oz) button mushrooms, sliced
4 chicken 'lovely legs' and 4 skinless thigh cutlets (see Note)
2 teaspoons cumin seeds
6 spring onions (scallions), sliced
500 ml (2 cups) chicken stock
140 g (¾ cup) brown lentils
2 tablespoons kecap manis

**1** Melt half the butter in a frying pan and quickly cook the mushrooms for 2–3 minutes, or until softened, then remove from the pan.
**2** Melt the remaining butter, add the chicken and cook for 3–4 minutes each side, or until brown. Add the cumin seeds and half the spring onion and cook for 1 minute. Add the stock and lentils and combine, making sure all the lentils are submerged. Bring to the boil, then reduce the heat and simmer, covered, for 30 minutes. Remove the lid and turn the chicken over, again making sure all the lentils are covered. Increase the heat and cook for a further 20 minutes, uncovered, allowing the stock to reduce. Check that the chicken is cooked and the lentils are tender.
**3** Stir through the kecap manis and the mushrooms, and season with salt and black pepper. Scatter with the remaining spring onions and serve with seared Roma (plum) tomatoes.

**NUTRITION PER SERVE**
Protein 47 g; Fat 17 g; Carbohydrate 14 g; Dietary Fibre 6 g; Cholesterol 140 mg; 1681 kJ (400 Cal)

### COOK'S FILE

**Note:** Lovely legs are drumsticks with the skin and lower leg bone removed.

1

2

3

## CURRIED CHICKEN WITH ALMONDS

Preparation time: 15 minutes
Total cooking time: 1 hour 30 minutes
Serves 4–6

1 tablespoon oil
1.5 kg (3 lb 5 oz) chicken pieces, on the bone
1 onion, finely chopped
2 cloves garlic, finely chopped
2 teaspoons grated fresh ginger
2½ tablespoons curry powder (see Note)
3 x 425 g (15 oz) cans tomatoes, drained and chopped
250 ml (1 cup) chicken stock
50 g (1¾ oz) slivered almonds, toasted

**1** Heat the oil in a saucepan, add the chicken, in batches, and cook for 3–4 minutes each side, or until brown. Remove the chicken from the pan.
**2** In the same pan, cook the onion, garlic and ginger for 2 minutes, or until soft. Add the curry powder and stir until fragrant. Add the tomato and simmer, stirring occasionally, for 10–15 minutes, or until the sauce is thick and pulpy.
**3** Stir in the stock and chicken. Simmer, covered, for 30–35 minutes and then uncovered for a further 30 minutes, or until the chicken is cooked and tender. Sprinkle with the almonds and serve with steamed rice.

**NUTRITION PER SERVE (6)**
Protein 45 g; Fat 17 g; Carbohydrate 6 g; Dietary Fibre 3 g; Cholesterol 140 mg; 1480 kJ (355 Cal)

### COOK'S FILE

**Note:** Curry powder is made up of a selection of ground spices, including coriander, fenugreek, cumin and mustard seeds, chilli, turmeric, ginger and cloves.

## CHICKEN STROGANOFF

Preparation time: 15 minutes
Total cooking time: 25 minutes
Serves 4

30 g (1 oz) butter
1 onion, finely sliced
2 cloves garlic, crushed
600 g (1 lb 5 oz) chicken tenderloins
180 g (2 cups) sliced button mushrooms
3 tablespoons tomato paste (purée)
300 g (10½ oz) sour cream

**1** Melt half the butter in a frying pan, add the onion and cook for 5 minutes, or until soft. Add the garlic and cook for 1 minute, then remove. Melt the remaining butter over high heat and brown the chicken in batches. Set aside with the onion mixture. Brown the mushrooms for 1–2 minutes.

**2** Return the onion mixture and chicken to the pan. Remove from the heat and stir in the tomato paste and sour cream. Return to the heat and cook, stirring constantly, until the mixture thickens. Reduce the heat and simmer for 5 minutes, or until the chicken is cooked through. Season and serve with pasta, steamed asparagus and snowpeas (mangetout).

**NUTRITION PER SERVE**
Protein 40 g; Fat 40 g; Carbohydrate 7.5 g; Dietary Fibre 2.5 g; Cholesterol 190 mg; 2255 kJ (540 Cal)

### COOK'S FILE

**Note:** If the tenderloins are very large, cut them in half lengthways.

## ASIAN RISSOLES

Preparation time: 15 minutes
Total cooking time: 30 minutes
Serves 4

600 g (1 lb 5 oz) minced (ground) chicken
2 tablespoons sweet chilli sauce
2 tablespoons coriander (cilantro), roughly chopped
2 stalks lemon grass, white part only, finely chopped
2 egg whites, lightly beaten
110 g (1 1/3 cups) fresh breadcrumbs
100 g (2/3 cup) sesame seeds
2–3 tablespoons oil

**1** Preheat the oven to 200°C (400°F/Gas 6). Combine the minced chicken, sweet chilli sauce, coriander, lemon grass, egg white and breadcrumbs. Season well with salt and pepper. Divide the mixture into 8 portions and shape into rissoles. Coat with the sesame seeds.
**2** Heat the oil in a frying pan and cook the rissoles, in batches, for 3–4 minutes each side, or until the crust is golden.
**3** Place the rissoles on a lined oven tray and bake for 15 minutes, or until cooked through. Serve the rissoles with a green salad and potato wedges or as a burger.

**NUTRITION PER SERVE**
Protein 45 g; Fat 33 g; Carbohydrate 20 g; Dietary Fibre 4 g; Cholesterol 75 mg; 2325 kJ (555 Cal)

## CHILLI CON POLLO

Preparation time: 10 minutes
Total cooking time: 45 minutes
Serves 4

1 tablespoon olive oil
1 onion, finely chopped
500 g (1 lb 2 oz) minced (ground) chicken
1–2 teaspoons mild chilli powder
440 g (1 lb) can chopped tomatoes
2 tablespoons tomato paste (purée)
1–2 teaspoons soft brown sugar
425 g (15 oz) can red kidney beans, rinsed and drained

**1** Heat the oil in a large saucepan. Add the onion and cook over medium heat for 3 minutes, or until soft. Increase the heat to high and add the chicken. Cook until browned, breaking up any lumps with a wooden spoon.

**2** Add the chilli powder and cook for 1 minute. Stir in the tomato, tomato paste and 125 ml ($1/2$ cup) water.

**3** Bring to the boil, then reduce the heat and simmer for 30 minutes. Stir through the sugar to taste and the kidney beans. Season. Serve with corn chips or in taco shells with sour cream.

**NUTRITION PER SERVE**
Protein 37 g; Fat 8.5 g; Carbohydrate 20 g; Dietary Fibre 9 g; Cholesterol 60 mg; 1305 kJ (312 Cal)

## CHICKEN MEATLOAF

Preparation time: 15 minutes
Total cooking time: 1 hour 15 minutes
Serves 4–6

1 kg (2 lb 4 oz) minced (ground) chicken
1 onion, grated
80 g (1 cup) fresh white breadcrumbs (2 slices day-old bread)
2 eggs, lightly beaten
80 ml ($1/3$ cup) barbecue sauce
2 tablespoons Worcestershire sauce
60 ml ($1/4$ cup) puréed tomato
2 tablespoons finely chopped flat-leaf (Italian) parsley

**1** Preheat the oven to 180°C (350°F/Gas 4). Combine the chicken, onion, breadcrumbs, egg, 2 tablespoons barbecue sauce, Worcestershire sauce, puréed tomato, parsley, salt and black pepper to taste, and mix well.
**2** Press into a lightly greased 1.5 litre (6 cup) loaf tin. Place on an oven tray to catch any juices that may spill over and bake for 1 hour.
**3** Pour off any excess fat from the tin. Spread the remaining barbecue sauce over the top of the meatloaf and bake for a further 15 minutes. Turn out the meatloaf and serve sliced with a salad and extra barbecue sauce, if desired.

NUTRITION PER SERVE (6)
Protein 40 g; Fat 6 g; Carbohydrate 15 g; Dietary Fibre 1 g; Cholesterol 145 mg; 1175 kJ (280 Cal)

### COOK'S FILE

**Note:** Meatloaf can be eaten hot or cold and is great to take on a picnic or to put in the kids' school sandwiches.

1

2

3

## MADRID CHICKEN

Preparation time: 10 minutes
Total cooking time: 1 hour
Serves 4

1 orange
1 tablespoon olive oil
4 chicken breasts on the bone, skin and excess fat removed
2 chorizo sausages (about 200 g/7 oz), cut into 1 cm ($^1/_2$ inch) slices (see Note)
250 ml (1 cup) chicken stock
250 ml (1 cup) bottled tomato pasta sauce
12 Kalamata olives
Kalamata olives, extra, to garnish
flat-leaf (Italian) parsley, to garnish

**1** Using a vegetable peeler, cut off 4 thin strips of orange zest. Remove the peel from the orange and segment.

**2** Heat the oil in a frying pan and brown the chicken and chorizo slices, in batches if necessary. (Leave the meat side of the chicken browning for 5 minutes.) Add the stock, tomato sauce and orange zest. Bring to the boil, then reduce the heat and simmer, covered, for 25 minutes.

**3** Remove the lid, turn the chicken over and continue to simmer, uncovered, for about 25 minutes, or until the chicken is tender and the sauce reduced. Season with salt and freshly ground black pepper and stir through the olives and reserved orange segments. Garnish with extra olives and flat-leaf parsley.

**NUTRITION PER SERVE**
Protein 75 g; Fat 30 g; Carbohydrate 12 g; Dietary Fibre 3.5 g; Cholesterol 250 mg; 2553 kJ (610 Cal)

### COOK'S FILE

**Note:** Chorizo sausages can be replaced with any spicy sausages.

1

2

3

## CHINESE BRAISED CHICKEN

Preparation time: 10 minutes
Total cooking time: 1 hour
Serves 4–6

250 ml (1 cup) soy sauce
1 cinnamon stick
90 g (1/3 cup) sugar
80 ml (1/3 cup) balsamic vinegar
2.5 cm (1 inch) piece fresh ginger, peeled and thinly sliced
4 garlic cloves
1/4 teaspoon chilli flakes
1.5 kg (3 lb 5 oz) chicken pieces on the bone (skin removed)
1 tablespoon toasted sesame seeds, to garnish

**1** Combine 1 litre (4 cups) water with the soy sauce, cinnamon, sugar, vinegar, ginger, garlic and chilli flakes in a saucepan. Bring to the boil, then reduce the heat and simmer for 5 minutes. Add the chicken and simmer, covered, for 50 minutes, or until cooked through. Serve on a bed of steamed greens, drizzled with the poaching liquid and sprinkled with toasted sesame seeds.

**NUTRITION PER SERVE (6)**
Protein 45 g; Fat 10 g; Carbohydrate 16 g; Dietary Fibre 0.5 g; Cholesterol 140 mg; 1420 kJ (339 Cal)

1

## ORANGE AND ROSEMARY GLAZED CHICKEN

Preparation time: 10 minutes
Total cooking time: 50 minutes
Serves 4–6

2 seedless oranges
175 g (1/2 cup) honey
1 1/2 tablespoons chopped rosemary
2 tablespoons Dijon mustard
4 cloves garlic, crushed
1.5 kg (3 lb 5 oz) chicken pieces, on the bone (skin on)
rosemary, to garnish

**1** Preheat the oven to 200°C (400°F/Gas 6). Line a large baking tray with foil. Squeeze the juice from one orange into a bowl, add the honey, rosemary, Dijon mustard and garlic, and mix together well. Cut the other orange in half and then into 1 cm (1/2 inch) slices.
**2** Add the chicken and orange slices to the orange juice mixture. Season and mix well. Arrange the chicken and the marinade in the baking tray.
**3** Bake for 40–50 minutes, or until the chicken is golden, turning and basting halfway through. Serve garnished with fresh rosemary.

NUTRITION PER SERVE (6)
Protein 40 g; Fat 8.5 g; Carbohydrate 27 g; Dietary Fibre 1 g; Cholesterol 138 mg; 1470 kJ (350 Cal)

### COOK'S FILE

**Note:** This recipe can be adapted with other flavour variations such as honey, soy and ginger, or honey, lemon and oregano. For maximum flavour, allow the chicken to marinate for up to 4 hours.

## OVEN 'FRIED' CHICKEN

Preparation time: 15 minutes
Total cooking time: 50 minutes
Serves 4–6

1.5 kg (3 lb 5 oz) chicken drumsticks
185 ml (3/4 cup) buttermilk
1 1/2 tablespoons olive oil
150 g (1 cup) polenta
100 g (1 cup) dry breadcrumbs
1/2 teaspoon chilli powder
2 eggs
40 g (1 1/2 oz) unsalted butter, melted

**1** Preheat the oven to 180°C (350°F/Gas 4). Grease a foil-lined baking tray. Place the drumsticks in a bowl, add the buttermilk and oil and toss to coat.
**2** In a separate bowl, combine the polenta, breadcrumbs and chilli powder, and season to taste with salt and freshly ground black pepper. Put the eggs in a small bowl and whisk with 1 tablespoon water.
**3** Dip the chicken in the egg mixture, then coat with the polenta mixture, pressing with your fingers to make the crumbs stick. Arrange on the baking tray and drizzle with melted butter. Bake for 45–50 minutes, or until the chicken is crisp and golden. Serve with sweet potato mash and a green salad.

**NUTRITION PER SERVE (6)**
Protein 55 g; Fat 25 g; Carbohydrate 25 g; Dietary Fibre 1 g; Cholesterol 285 mg; 2377 kJ (568 Cal)

### COOK'S FILE

**Note:** Oven-frying delivers a crisp, crunchy crust with a lot less fat than traditional deep-frying. For an even leaner version, remove the skin from the chicken before coating. To make the 'fried' chicken really moist, marinate the drumsticks in the buttermilk and oil for up to 8 hours.

1

2

3

## CHICKEN AND RICE WITH GREEN CAPSICUM AND TOMATOES

Preparation time: 15 minutes
Total cooking time: 1 hour
Serves 4–6

1½ tablespoons olive oil
1.2 kg (2 lb 11 oz) chicken pieces
1 onion, finely chopped
2 green capsicums (peppers), diced
3 cloves garlic, crushed
2 tablespoons paprika
300 g (1½ cups) long- or medium-grain rice
2 x 425 g (15 oz) cans diced tomatoes

**1** Heat the oil in a large saucepan over high heat, add the chicken, skin-side down, and cook for 4 minutes each side, or until well browned. Drain the chicken on paper towels. Pour all but 1½ tablespoons of fat from the pan.

**2** Reduce the heat to medium, add the onion and capsicum and cook for about 3–4 minutes, or until soft. Add the garlic, paprika and rice, and cook for a further 1 minute.

**3** Add the tomato and 560 ml (2¼ cups) water, scraping any browned bits off the pan with a wooden spoon. Return the chicken to the pan and bring to the boil. Reduce the heat and simmer, covered, for 50 minutes, stirring occasionally to prevent sticking. Season and serve.

**NUTRITION PER SERVE (6)**
Protein 36 g; Fat 12 g; Carbohydrate 45 g; Dietary Fibre 3.5 g; Cholesterol 100 mg; 1830 kJ (435 Cal)

## STUFFED CHICKEN MARYLANDS

Preparation time: 15 minutes
Total cooking time: 55 minutes
Serves 4

80 ml (1/3 cup) olive oil
2 onions, finely chopped
4 cloves garlic, finely chopped
100 g (1 cup) dry breadcrumbs
zest of 2 lemons, finely grated
2 tablespoons lemon juice
4 tablespoons chopped basil
4 chicken Maryland (leg quarter) pieces

**1** Preheat the oven to 200°C (400°F/Gas 6). Heat the oil in a frying pan and cook the onion for 4–5 minutes, or until soft. Add the garlic and breadcrumbs and cook, stirring, for 3–4 minutes, or until the breadcrumbs begin to turn light brown. Remove from the heat and stir in the lemon zest, lemon juice and basil, and season.
**2** With your fingers, loosen the skin from the Maryland, including the leg, to form a pocket. Carefully place about 3 tablespoons of the stuffing under the skin of each Maryland, pressing gently to flatten it. Season.
**3** Bake on a lightly greased baking tray for 45 minutes, or until the skin is tender and the meat firm to the touch. Serve with red onion and grilled (broiled) pear.

**NUTRITION PER SERVE**
Protein 60 g; Fat 25 g; Carbohydrate 23 g; Dietary Fibre 2.5 g; Cholesterol 120 mg; 2357 kJ (565 Cal)

## PENNE WITH SAUTEED CHICKEN, ASPARAGUS AND GOATS CHEESE

Preparation time: 15 minutes
Total cooking time: 35 minutes
Serves 4

500 g (1 lb 2 oz) penne pasta
350 g (12 oz) fresh asparagus spears
1 tablespoon olive oil
2 chicken breast fillets, cut into 3 cm (1¼ inch) cubes
1 tablespoon finely chopped thyme
250 ml (1 cup) chicken stock
80 ml (⅓ cup) balsamic vinegar
150 g (5½ oz) goats cheese

**1** Bring a large saucepan of salted water to the boil, add the pasta and cook for 10–12 minutes, or until *al dente*. Drain and keep warm.

**2** Remove the woody ends from the asparagus, cut into short lengths and cook in a pan of boiling water for 3 minutes, or until just tender.

**3** Heat the oil in a pan over high heat. Add the chicken and cook in batches for 5 minutes, or until browned. Return the chicken to the pan. Add the thyme and cook for 1 minute. Add the stock and vinegar and bring to the boil. Reduce the heat and simmer, stirring, for 3–4 minutes, or until the sauce has reduced slightly, then add the asparagus. Toss the pasta with the chicken in a serving bowl and crumble the cheese over the top. Season and serve.

**NUTRITION PER SERVE**
Protein 45 g; Fat 17 g; Carbohydrate 90 g; Dietary Fibre 7.5 g; Cholesterol 75 mg; 2957 kJ (705 Cal)

### COOK'S FILE

**Variation:** Feta cheese can be substituted for the goats cheese.

## BRAISED CHICKEN IN WINE AND LEEKS

Preparation time: 15 minutes
Total cooking time: 1 hour
Serves 4

2 tablespoons oil
1.2 kg (2 lb 11 oz) chicken pieces
1 leek, thinly sliced
5 spring onions (scallions), cut thinly on the diagonal
2 tablespoons marjoram
150 ml (5 fl oz) white wine
400 ml (14 fl oz) chicken stock
100 ml (3½ fl oz) cream

**1** Score the chicken drumsticks. Heat 1 tablespoon oil in a frying pan and cook the chicken pieces, in batches, for 3–4 minutes, or until browned.

**2** Heat the remaining oil in a large casserole dish and cook the leek, spring onion and marjoram for 4 minutes, or until soft. Add the chicken and wine, and cook for 2 minutes. Add the stock, cover and bring to the boil. Reduce the heat and simmer for 30 minutes. Stir in the cream and simmer, uncovered, for 15 minutes, or until the chicken is tender. Season. Serve with steamed rice.

**NUTRITION PER SERVE**
Protein 48 g; Fat 30 g; Carbohydrate 2.5 g; Dietary Fibre 1 g; Cholesterol 190 mg; 2065 kJ (493 Cal)

## SPICY APRICOT CHICKEN

Preparation time: 10 minutes
Total cooking time: 20 minutes
Serves 4

750 g (1 lb 10 oz) chicken thigh fillets, cut into 5 cm (2 inch) pieces
plain (all-purpose) flour, for coating
2 tablespoons oil
2 teaspoons red curry paste
2 spring onions (scallions), sliced
415 g (15 oz) can apricot halves in light syrup
125 ml ($1/2$ cup) chicken stock
200 g (7 oz) plain yoghurt
2 tablespoons chopped coriander (cilantro) leaves

**1** Lightly coat the chicken in the flour. Heat the oil in a saucepan, add the curry paste and stir over low heat for 1 minute. Add the spring onion and chicken and cook, stirring, over medium heat for 2–3 minutes, or until the chicken is golden.
**2** Drain the apricots and reserve 125 ml ($1/2$ cup) of the juice. Add the reserved juice, apricots and chicken stock to the pan. Bring to the boil, then reduce the heat and simmer for 10 minutes, or until the chicken is tender.
**3** Mix together the yoghurt and coriander and place a spoonful of the mixture over each serving of chicken. Serve with couscous or rice.

**NUTRITION PER SERVE**
Protein 45 g; Fat 15 g; Carbohydrate 15 g; Dietary Fibre 2 g; Cholesterol 100 mg; 1622 kJ (388 Cal)

1

2

## GLAZED CHICKEN LEGS

Preparation time: 10 minutes
Total cooking time: 1 hour 5 minutes
Serves 4

8 chicken drumsticks
125 ml (1/2 cup) orange juice concentrate
80 ml (1/3 cup) kecap manis
2 tablespoons oil
1 tablespoon sesame oil
2 teaspoons Chinese five-spice powder
3 cloves garlic, crushed
lime wedges, to garnish

**1** Preheat the oven to 180°C (350°F/Gas 4). Place the chicken in a saucepan of cold water. Bring to the boil, then reduce the heat and simmer, covered, for 15 minutes. Drain.

**2** Whisk the orange concentrate, kecap manis, oil, sesame oil, Chinese five-spice and garlic together in a bowl. Put the chicken in a large ovenproof dish and pour the marinade over, coating the chicken.

**3** Cover the chicken with foil and bake for 50 minutes, or until tender, turning once during cooking. Baste the chicken while cooking. Serve with lime wedges and a green salad.

**NUTRITION PER SERVE**
Protein 25 g; Fat 20 g; Carbohydrate 4 g; Dietary Fibre 0.5 g; Cholesterol 100 mg; 1260 kJ (300 Cal)

1

2

3

## CHICKEN WITH PEAS AND BACON

Preparation time: 10 minutes
Total cooking time: 35 minutes
Serves 4–6

2 tablespoons olive oil
1 onion, chopped
4 bacon rashers, fat removed, cut into strips
800 g (1 lb 12 oz) chicken tenderloins
125 ml ($^1/_2$ cup) dry white wine
125 ml ($^1/_2$ cup) chicken stock
1 tablespoon sage, finely chopped
300 g (10$^1/_2$ oz) frozen peas

**1** Heat the oil in a frying pan over high heat. Add the onion and bacon and cook, stirring constantly, for 2 minutes, or until the onion is soft, then remove.
**2** Season the chicken and cook, in batches, turning often, for 3–4 minutes, or until browned evenly.
**3** Add the wine, stock, bacon and onion, and sage, and bring to the boil. Reduce the heat and simmer, covered, for 20 minutes. Add the peas and cook, uncovered, for a further 5 minutes, or until soft. Season with salt and freshly ground black pepper and serve with mash or polenta.

**NUTRITION PER SERVE (6)**
Protein 35 g; Fat 10 g; Carbohydrate 5 g; Dietary Fibre 3 g; Cholesterol 75 mg; 1165 kJ (280 Cal)

### COOK'S FILE

**Note:** Tenderloins can be substituted with breast fillets if unavailable.

1

2

## CHICKEN CARBONARA

Preparation time: 10 minutes
Total cooking time: 20 minutes
Serves 4

350 g (12 oz) dried or 500 g (1 lb 2 oz) fresh tomato fettucine
600 g (1 lb 5 oz) chicken tenderloins
40 g (1½ oz) butter
3 eggs
300 ml (10½ fl oz) cream
50 g (½ cup) freshly grated Parmesan cheese
shaved Parmesan cheese
basil leaves, to garnish

**1** Bring a saucepan of salted water to the boil. Add the fettucine and cook according to the packet instructions, or until *al dente*. Drain and keep warm.
**2** Trim and slice the tenderloins in half on the diagonal. Melt the butter in a frying pan and cook the chicken for 4–5 minutes, or until browned. Lightly beat the eggs and cream together and stir in the grated Parmesan. Season with salt to taste and stir through the chicken.
**3** Combine the chicken and cream mixture with the fettucine in the frying pan. Reduce the heat and cook, stirring constantly, for 10–15 seconds, or until the sauce is slightly thickened. Do not keep on the heat too long or the eggs will set and scramble. Season with black pepper and serve, garnished with the extra Parmesan and basil leaves.

**NUTRITION PER SERVE**
Protein 54 g; Fat 52 g; Carbohydrate 64 g; Dietary Fibre 4.5 g; Cholesterol 348 mg; 3927 kJ (938 Cal)

### COOK'S FILE

**Variation:** Saffron fettucine is a delicious substitute for tomato fettucine.

## CHICKEN WITH BALSAMIC VINEGAR

Preparation time: 5 minutes
Total cooking time: 40 minutes
Serves 4

2 tablespoons olive oil
8 (1.2 kg/2 lb 11 oz) chicken pieces
125 ml (1/2 cup) chicken stock
125 ml (1/2 cup) dry white wine
125 ml (1/2 cup) balsamic vinegar
40 g (1 1/2 oz) cold butter

**1** Heat the oil in a large casserole dish over medium heat and cook the chicken, in batches, for 7–8 minutes, or until browned. Pour off any excess fat.

**2** Add the stock, bring to the boil, then reduce the heat and simmer, covered, for 30 minutes, or until the chicken is cooked through.

**3** Add the white wine and vinegar and increase the heat to high. Boil for 1 minute, or until thickened. Remove from the heat, stir in the butter until melted, and season. Spoon the sauce over the chicken to serve, with roast potatoes and salad.

**NUTRITION PER SERVE**
Protein 40 g; Fat 25 g; Carbohydrate 0.5 g; Dietary Fibre 0 g; Cholesterol 165 mg; 1790 kJ (430 Cal)

### COOK'S FILE

**Note:** Use the best-quality balsamic vinegar you can afford, as the cheaper varieties can be too acidic.

# SPECIAL OCCASION DINING

### COQ AU VIN

Preparation time: 15 minutes
Total cooking time: 1 hour 40 minutes
Serves 4–6

30 g (1 oz) butter
125 g (4½ oz) bacon, chopped
1.5 kg (3 lb 5 oz) skinless chicken pieces
350 g (12 oz) baby onions
2 tablespoons plain (all-purpose) flour
750 ml (3 cups) red wine
250 g (9 oz) field mushrooms, sliced
1 tablespoon thyme leaves

**1** Preheat the oven to 180°C (350°F/Gas 4). Melt the butter in a large ovenproof casserole dish. Add the bacon and cook until golden, then remove. Add the chicken and cook, in batches, for 4–5 minutes, or until browned. Remove. Add the onions and cook for 2–3 minutes, or until browned, then remove from the pan.
**2** Stir in the flour to the pan, remove from the heat and slowly pour in the wine, while stirring. Return to the heat, bring to the boil and return the bacon and chicken to the pan. Cover and bake for 1 hour. Return the onions to the pan and add the mushrooms. Cook for a further 30 minutes. Season with salt and freshly ground black pepper and garnish with the thyme. Serve with mashed potato, if desired.

**NUTRITION PER SERVE (6)**
Protein 65 g; Fat 11 g; Carbohydrate 11 g; Dietary Fibre 2 g; Cholesterol 150 mg; 2040 kJ (487 Cal)

## LIME STEAMED CHICKEN

Preparation time: 15 minutes
Total cooking time: 15 minutes
Serves 4

2 limes, thinly sliced
4 chicken breast fillets
550 g (1 lb 4 oz) bok choy (pak choi)
550 g (1 lb 4 oz) choy sum
1 teaspoon sesame oil
1 tablespoon peanut oil
125 ml ($^1/_2$ cup) oyster sauce
80 ml ($^1/_3$ cup) lime juice
lime slices, extra, to garnish

**1** Line the base of a bamboo steamer with the lime and place the chicken on top and season. Place over a wok with a little water in the base, cover and steam for 8–10 minutes, or until the chicken is cooked through. Cover the chicken and keep warm. Remove the water from the wok.
**2** Wash and trim the greens. Heat the oils in the wok and cook the greens for 2–3 minutes, or until just wilted.
**3** Combine the oyster sauce and lime juice and pour over the greens when they are cooked. Place the chicken on serving plates on top of the greens and serve with steamed rice and lime slices.

### NUTRITION PER SERVE
Protein 60 g; Fat 12 g; Carbohydrate 10 g; Dietary Fibre 4.5 g; Cholesterol 120 mg; 1665 kJ (398 Cal)

### COOK'S FILE

**Note:** The vegetables used in this recipe can be replaced by any green vegetables, such as broccoli, snowpeas (mangetout), or English spinach.

1

2

3

# THAI COCONUT CHICKEN

Preparation time: 10 minutes
Total cooking time: 45 minutes
Serves 4

1 tablespoon peanut oil
6 spring onions (scallions), sliced
2 tablespoons green curry paste
400 ml (14 fl oz) can coconut milk
8 chicken thigh cutlets, skin removed
1 teaspoon finely grated lime zest
1 tablespoon lime juice
1 tablespoon fish sauce
7 g ($1/4$ cup) coriander (cilantro) leaves

**1** Heat the oil in a saucepan, add the spring onion and curry paste and cook, stirring, for 2 minutes. Add the coconut milk and 125 ml ($1/2$ cup) water and bring to the boil.

**2** Reduce the heat, add the chicken thigh cutlets and lime zest, and simmer for 35–40 minutes, or until the chicken is cooked through. Stir through the lime juice, fish sauce and coriander leaves. Serve with steamed jasmine rice.

**NUTRITION PER SERVE**
Protein 25 g; Fat 30 g; Carbohydrate 5 g; Dietary Fibre 2 g; Cholesterol 103 mg; 1717 kJ (410 Cal)

### COOK'S FILE

**Note:** Chicken thigh fillets can be used if thigh cutlets are unavailable.

## INDIVIDUAL CHICKEN AND MUSHROOM PIES

Preparation time: 15 minutes
 + refrigeration
Total cooking time: 55 minutes
Serves 4

60 g (2¼ oz) butter
2 leeks, chopped
6 chicken thigh fillets, cut into 2 cm (¾ inch) cubes
270 g (9½ oz) button mushrooms, halved
2 tablespoons plain (all-purpose) flour
600 ml (2½ cups) chicken stock
1–2 sheets ready-rolled puff pastry, thawed
1 egg yolk

**1** Melt the butter in a frying pan and cook the leek for 3–4 minutes, or until soft. Add the chicken and cook for 2 minutes, then add the mushrooms and cook for 4 minutes. Stir in the flour and cook for 30 seconds. Remove from the heat and gradually pour in the stock. Cook for 2 minutes to thicken and then remove from the heat. Place in a bowl, cover with plastic wrap, and cool in the fridge.
**2** Preheat the oven to 200°C (400°F/Gas 6). Lightly grease four 315 ml (1¼ cup) ovenproof dishes. Cut four pastry rounds to cover the tops.
**3** Spoon the cooled chicken mixture into the prepared dishes, fill to the top and cover with the pastry lid, sealing the edges with a fork. Brush each lid with egg yolk and, using a sharp knife, make a cut in the pastry to allow steam to escape. Bake on a tray in the oven for 30–40 minutes, or until the pastry is golden and cooked. Serve with peas and mashed potato, if desired.

**NUTRITION PER SERVE**
Protein 50 g; Fat 22 g; Carbohydrate 7 g; Dietary Fibre 3 g; Cholesterol 190 mg; 1761 kJ (420 Cal)

### COOK'S FILE

**Hint:** Make the filling a day in advance so it has time to cool properly before being put into the dishes.

## CHICKEN TARTS WITH PUMPKIN, SPINACH AND HALOUMI

Preparation time: 20 minutes
Total cooking time: 55 minutes
Serves 4

430 g (15 oz) pumpkin, cut into 5 mm ($^1/_4$ inch) slices
3 tablespoons olive oil
2 chicken breast fillets
120 g ($4^1/_2$ oz) haloumi cheese
1 sheet puff pastry, defrosted and cut into four 12 x 12 cm (5 x 5 inch) squares
35 g ($1^1/_4$ oz) baby English spinach leaves

**1** Preheat the oven to 200°C (400°F/Gas 6). Put the pumpkin on a baking tray and brush with 1 tablespoon oil. Season with pepper. Bake in the oven for 15–20 minutes, or until the pumpkin is soft.
**2** Heat 1 tablespoon oil in a frying pan and cook the chicken for 5 minutes on each side, or until cooked through. Cut each breast into 8 slices to give 16 pieces. Cut the haloumi into 8 slices and cut each slice in half.
**3** Place the pastry squares on a lined oven tray. Lay the pieces of pumpkin over the base of the tarts, leaving a 1 cm ($^1/_2$ inch) border. Place the spinach leaves over the top, then the chicken pieces and the sliced haloumi. Brush with the remaining oil. Bake for 25 minutes, or until the base of the pastry is cooked and the top is golden and the pastry is puffed.

**NUTRITION PER SERVE**
Protein 48 g; Fat 35 g; Carbohydrate 22 g; Dietary Fibre 2 g; Cholesterol 110 mg; 2428 kJ (580 Cal)

## STEAMED CHICKEN WITH CORIANDER PESTO

Preparation time: 15 minutes + 10 minutes standing
Total cooking time: 20 minutes
Serves 4

4 chicken breast fillets
90 g (3 cups) coriander (cilantro)
2 teaspoons ground cumin
1 small red chilli
2 cloves garlic
zest of 2 lemons, grated
80 ml (1/3 cup) lemon juice
80 ml (1/3 cup) olive oil
185 g (1 cup) couscous
lemon zest, extra, to garnish

**1** Place the chicken fillets in a bamboo or metal steamer and steam for 15–20 minutes, or until cooked through. Remove and thinly slice. Set aside and keep warm.

**2** To make the coriander pesto, place the coriander, cumin, chilli, garlic, half the lemon zest, 2 tablespoons lemon juice and 2 tablespoons olive oil in a food processor, and process until smooth. Season to taste.

**3** Put the couscous in a saucepan and add 500 ml (2 cups) boiling water. Add the remaining oil, lemon zest and lemon juice. Stir off the heat. Cover and leave to stand for 10 minutes. Remove the lid and fluff the couscous with a fork. Season well. To serve, put the couscous on a plate, top with the chicken and a spoonful of the coriander pesto. Garnish with extra lemon zest, if desired.

**NUTRITION PER SERVE**
Protein 53 g; Fat 25 g; Carbohydrate 27 g; Dietary Fibre 1.5 g; Cholesterol 110 mg; 2295 kJ (550 Cal)

### COOK'S FILE

**Note:** The chicken can be pan-fried or grilled instead, but will need to be basted to avoid drying out.

## CORIANDER AND LIME CHICKEN

Preparation time: 10 minutes
Total cooking time: 15 minutes
Serves 4

160 g (²/₃ cup) coconut cream
125 ml (¹/₂ cup) chicken stock
1¹/₂ tablespoons lime juice
2 teaspoons grated fresh ginger
4 chicken breast fillets
plain (all-purpose) flour, for dusting
2 tablespoons oil
2 tablespoons chopped coriander (cilantro) leaves
coriander (cilantro) leaves, extra, to garnish

**1** Whisk the coconut cream, stock, lime juice and ginger together in a medium bowl. Cut the chicken across the grain into 1 cm (¹/₂ inch) slices and lightly coat with flour.
**2** Heat the oil in a frying pan and cook the chicken over medium heat for 4–5 minutes, or until golden brown. Remove from the pan and keep warm. Add the coconut cream mixture to the pan and bring to the boil. Cook for 5 minutes, or until the sauce is reduced by half and thickened slightly.
**3** Return the chicken strips to the pan, add the coriander and simmer for 1 minute to heat the chicken through. Garnish with the extra coriander leaves. Serve with steamed jasmine rice.

**NUTRITION PER SERVE**
Protein 50 g; Fat 20 g; Carbohydrate 13 g; Dietary Fibre 1 g; Cholesterol 110 mg; 1785 kJ (425 Cal)

### COOK'S FILE

**Variation:** Sprinkle with chopped red chilli and serve with stir-fried carrot strips and snowpeas (mangetout).

## CHICKEN BREAST WITH BALSAMIC RELISH

Preparation time: 15 minutes
Total cooking time: 25 minutes
Serves 4

3 tablespoons olive oil
2 small red capsicums (peppers), cut into 2 cm ($^3/_4$ inch) pieces
2 red onions, cut into large pieces
150 g ($5^1/_2$ oz) marinated green olives, seeded
3–4 tablespoons balsamic vinegar
3–4 tablespoons soft brown sugar
4 chicken breast fillets

**1** To make the balsamic relish, heat 2 tablespoons of the oil in a saucepan over medium heat, add the capsicum and onion and cook for 5 minutes. Add the olives and stir in the vinegar and sugar to taste. Cook for another 20 minutes, or until the vegetables are soft and the liquid is syrupy.
**2** While the relish is cooking, heat the remaining oil in a frying pan and add the chicken. Cook over medium heat for 5 minutes on each side, or until the chicken is cooked through. Season and cut into thick slices on the diagonal. Serve the chicken on the relish with creamy mashed potato on the side.

NUTRITION PER SERVE
Protein 53 g; Fat 20 g; Carbohydrate 27 g; Dietary Fibre 3.5 g; Cholesterol 110 mg; 2115 kJ (505 Cal)

### COOK'S FILE

**Note:** The relish can be made in advance and, if you have any left, can be kept in the refrigerator in a clean jar for several weeks.

## SATAY CHICKEN WITH MANGO

Preparation time: 10 minutes
Total cooking time: 15 minutes
Serves 4

80 ml (1/3 cup) satay sauce
125 ml (1/2 cup) coconut cream
125 ml (1/2 cup) chicken stock
2 teaspoons soy sauce
500 g (1 lb 2 oz) chicken tenderloins
3 tablespoons plain (all-purpose) flour
2 tablespoons oil
1 large ripe mango, sliced

**1** Whisk the satay sauce, coconut cream, chicken stock and soy sauce together in a bowl.

**2** Lightly coat the chicken with flour. Heat the oil in a large deep frying pan and cook the chicken over medium heat for 4–5 minutes, or until golden brown. Remove from the pan and keep warm.

**3** Add the satay sauce mixture to the pan and bring to the boil. Boil for 3–5 minutes, or until the sauce is reduced by half. Return the chicken to the pan and heat through for 1 minute. Serve the chicken over steamed rice and top with mango slices.

**NUTRITION PER SERVE**
Protein 30 g; Fat 25 g; Carbohydrate 17 g; Dietary Fibre 2 g; Cholesterol 70 mg; 1710 kJ (410 Cal)

### COOK'S FILE

**Note:** Chicken breast fillets cut into strips work just as well as tenderloins in this recipe.

## GRUYERE CHICKEN

Preparation time: 10 minutes
Total cooking time: 15 minutes
Serves 4

4 chicken breast fillets, flattened (see Note)
plain (all-purpose) flour, for dusting
2 tablespoons olive oil
125 g (4½ oz) button mushrooms, sliced
3 spring onions (scallions), sliced
125 ml (½ cup) cream
1 tablespoon brandy
100 g (¾ cup) grated Gruyère or Swiss cheese

**1** Dust the chicken breasts with flour. Heat the oil in a frying pan and cook the chicken for 4–5 minutes each side, or until golden brown. Transfer to a lined oven tray and cover with foil.
**2** Add the mushrooms and spring onion to the pan. Cook for 2 minutes, or until the spring onion is soft. Add the cream and brandy and bring to the boil. Reduce the heat and simmer for 1 minute, or until the sauce reduces slightly. Season.
**3** Spoon the sauce over the chicken and top with the cheese. Place under a hot griller (broiler) until the cheese melts. Serve with roasted vegetables.

NUTRITION PER SERVE
Protein 60 g; Fat 35 g; Carbohydrate 10 g; Dietary Fibre 1.5 g; Cholesterol 175 mg; 2553 kJ (610 Cal)

### COOK'S FILE

**Note:** Flatten the chicken breast fillets by placing them between two pieces of plastic wrap and pressing down with the palm of your hand.

1

2

3

## CHICKEN BREAST STUFFED WITH SPINACH AND FETA

Preparation time: 15 minutes
Total cooking time: 15 minutes
Serves 4

4 chicken breast fillets
1 tablespoon olive oil
2 cloves garlic, crushed
250 g (9 oz) English spinach, stems removed
125 g (4½ oz) feta cheese, crumbled
2 teaspoons lemon zest
40 g (¼ cup) semi-dried (sun-blushed) tomatoes, chopped
2 tablespoons oil

**1** Butterfly the chicken fillets with a sharp knife by slicing horizontally through the middle. Do not cut all the way through.
**2** Heat the olive oil in a large saucepan over medium heat. Add the garlic and cook for 1 minute, or until fragrant. Wash the spinach and add to the pan with just the water clinging to the leaves. Cover the pan for about 1 minute, or until the spinach has wilted. Remove the lid and simmer for 1–2 minutes, or until most of the liquid has evaporated. Remove from the pan and roughly chop. Stir in the feta, lemon zest and semi-dried tomato. Mix together well.
**3** Open up one of the chicken breasts and place a quarter of the spinach mixture in the centre and along the length. Fold over the chicken to cover the mixture and secure with toothpicks. Repeat with the remaining fillets. Heat the oil in a large frying pan over medium heat, add the chicken and cook for 4–5 minutes each side, or until cooked through and golden brown. Cut into thick slices and serve over steamed green beans and Kalamata olives. Sprinkle with sea salt.

**NUTRITION PER SERVE**
Protein 57 g; Fat 27 g; Carbohydrate 1 g; Dietary Fibre 2 g; Cholesterol 130 mg; 1977 kJ (470 Cal)

## PECAN-CRUSTED CHICKEN

Preparation time: 15 minutes +
  30 minutes refrigeration
Total cooking time: 40 minutes
Serves 6

75 g (2½ oz) whole pecans, finely chopped
120 g (1½ cups) fresh breadcrumbs
7 g (¼ cup) chopped flat-leaf (Italian) parsley
3 teaspoons onion powder
1½ teaspoons garlic powder
2 teaspoons paprika
12 chicken thigh cutlets
1 tablespoon olive oil

**1** Combine the pecans, breadcrumbs, parsley, onion powder, garlic powder, paprika and 1½ teaspoons salt in a freezer bag and shake well.

**2** Put the chicken thigh cutlets in the freezer bag with the breadcrumb mixture and shake well to cover the chicken with the crumbs. Place the chicken on a greased oven tray, cover and leave in the refrigerator for at least 30 minutes to allow the crumbs to stick, or overnight if time permits, to let the flavours develop fully.

**3** Preheat the oven to 180°C (350°F/Gas 4). Drizzle the chicken with oil and bake for 35–40 minutes, or until the chicken is cooked and has a golden crust. Serve with shredded red cabbage and lime wedges.

**NUTRITION PER SERVE**
Protein 50 g; Fat 23 g; Carbohydrate 15 g; Dietary Fibre 2 g; Cholesterol 210 mg; 1990 kJ (476 Cal)

### COOK'S FILE

**Variation:** Finely chopped pistachio nuts or almonds can be substituted for the pecans.

## CHICKEN ROLLS WITH CREAMY MUSHROOM AND PEPPERCORN SAUCE

Preparation time: 15 minutes
Total cooking time: 20 minutes
Serves 4

4 green beans, blanched
1 carrot, julienned and blanched
4 chicken breast fillets, flattened
2 tablespoons oil
1 small onion, diced
100 g (3½ oz) button mushrooms, sliced
300 ml (10½ fl oz) thick (double/heavy) cream
3 teaspoons canned or bottled green peppercorns, lightly crushed

**1** Divide the beans and carrots into four and place in the centre of the breast fillets to create a filling. Roll the fillets and secure with a toothpick.
**2** Heat the oil in a large saucepan and cook the rolls over medium heat, turning as they cook, for 10 minutes, or until cooked through and golden. Remove from the pan and keep warm.
**3** To make the sauce, in the same pan, cook the onion and mushrooms for 2–3 minutes, or until the onion is soft. Add the cream and peppercorns and stir to combine. Simmer for 5 minutes, or until the sauce thickens slightly. Remove the toothpicks from the chicken and cut each roll into four on the diagonal. Spoon the sauce onto the plate and top with the chicken slices. Season with salt and freshly ground black pepper and serve with steamed asparagus.

**NUTRITION PER SERVE**
Protein 12 g; Fat 42 g; Carbohydrate 15 g; Dietary Fibre 5 g; Cholesterol 113 mg; 2000 kJ (478 Cal)

## COCONUT CHILLI CHICKEN

Preparation time: 20 minutes + overnight marinating
Total cooking time: 1 hour
Serves 4–6

1.6 kg (3 lb 8 oz) whole chicken (see Note)
1 small onion, chopped
1 tablespoon grated fresh ginger
3 cloves garlic, chopped
2 teaspoons ground cumin
2 small red chillies, chopped
270 ml (9½ fl oz) can coconut milk
15 g (¼ cup) finely chopped coriander (cilantro) leaves

**1** Prepare the chicken by removing the backbone with a pair of kitchen shears. Wash in cold water and pat dry with paper towels. Flatten the chicken out by pushing on the breast.

**2** To make the marinade, place the onion, ginger, garlic, cumin and chilli in a food processor and process until combined. Place in a bowl and add the coconut milk and coriander.

**3** Put the chicken in a plastic bag or a non-metallic bowl and pour the coconut chilli marinade over it. Ensure the chicken is well coated. Seal the bag and leave to marinate overnight.

**4** Preheat the oven to 200°C (400°F/Gas 6). Place the chicken on a greased oven tray, spoon on any excess marinade and bake for 1 hour, or until cooked through and crispy. Allow to stand for 10 minutes before cutting into pieces. Serve with Asian-style salad greens or on a bed of rice.

**NUTRITION PER SERVE (6)**
Protein 36 g; Fat 16 g; Carbohydrate 2.5 g; Dietary Fibre 1.5 g; Cholesterol 115 mg; 1245 kJ (300 Cal)

**COOK'S FILE**

**Note:** You can ask your butcher to remove the chicken backbone for you.

1

2

3

4

## ROAST LEMON AND CHIVE CHICKEN

Preparation time: 10 minutes
Total cooking time: 1 hour 30 minutes
Serves 4

60 g (2¼ oz) butter
1.5 kg (3 lb 5 oz) whole chicken
zest of 1 lemon, finely grated
60 ml (¼ cup) lemon juice
125 ml (½ cup) chicken stock
4 tablespoons snipped chives

**1** Preheat the oven to 200°C (400°F/Gas 6). Melt 15 g (½ oz) butter and brush over the chicken. Sprinkle the lemon zest over the chicken.
**2** Place the chicken in a baking dish with 125 ml (½ cup) water. Cook in the oven for 1 hour 15 minutes, or until the chicken is cooked through and the juices are clear when the chicken is pierced by a skewer. Remove from the baking dish and set aside in a warm place for 10–15 minutes.
**3** Pour off any excess fat from the baking dish and stir in the lemon juice and stock, scraping up the browned cooking juices. Place the baking dish over low heat and add the remaining butter a little at a time, whisking as you add it. Add the chives and pour the sauce into a serving bowl to accompany the chicken when carved. Serve with potato wedges and vegetables.

**NUTRITION PER SERVE**
Protein 60 g; Fat 25 g; Carbohydrate 1 g; Dietary Fibre 0 g; Cholesterol 245 mg; 2010 kJ (480 Cal)

## QUICK SHORT CHICKEN RECIPES

### CHICKEN WITH GARLIC AND HERB BUTTER

Preparation time: 15 minutes + refrigeration
Total cooking time: 15 minutes
Serves 4

60 g (2¼ oz) butter, softened
2 cloves garlic, crushed
1½ tablespoons chopped flat-leaf (Italian) parsley
1 tablespoon chopped oregano
4 chicken breast fillets
2 tablespoons oil

**1** To make the garlic and herb butter, combine the butter, garlic, parsley and oregano in a bowl. Place the mixture onto a sheet of baking paper and roll into a log shape. Twist the ends of the paper in opposite directions, giving the log a nice symmetrical shape. Put the log in the refrigerator until it hardens.

**2** Cover the chicken breasts with plastic wrap and flatten with your hand, a rolling pin or a meat mallet. Season with salt and freshly ground black pepper. Heat the oil in a frying pan, add the chicken and cook over medium heat for 10–15 minutes, or until golden brown and cooked through, turning once.

**3** Remove the butter log from the refrigerator and cut it into 1 cm (½ inch) slices. To serve, place the chicken on a plate and, while still hot, top with a slice of the garlic and herb butter. The butter will melt over the chicken. Serve the chicken hot with grilled vegetables.

**NUTRITION PER SERVE**
Protein 50 g; Fat 25 g; Carbohydrate 0 g; Dietary Fibre 0.5 g; Cholesterol 150 mg; 1850 kJ (440 Cal)

### COOK'S FILE

**Note:** The garlic and herb butter log can be prepared a few days in advance and refrigerated, or kept in the freezer for up to 1 month.

1

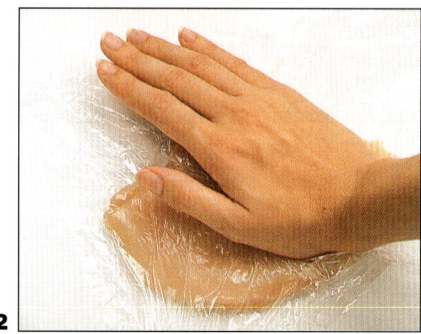

2

3

# INDEX

almonds, Curried chicken with, 76
apricot chicken, Spicy, 89
artichoke pizza, Chicken &, 69
Asian barbecued chicken, 63
Asian chicken noodle soup, 7
Asian rissoles, 78
asparagus & goats cheese, Penne with sautéed chicken, 87
asparagus stir-fry, Chicken &, 37

bacon, Chicken with peas &, 91
bagel burger, Chicken, 21
Baked chicken & leek risotto, 73
balsamic relish, Chicken breast with, 102
balsamic vinegar, Chicken with, 93
barbecues & grills
 Asian barbecued chicken, 63
 Blackened Cajun spiced chicken, 61
 Chargrilled chicken salad with rocket & cannellini beans, 51
 Chermoula chicken, 60
 Chicken tikka kebabs, 56
 Chicken wings marinated in soy, 52
 Chicken with yoghurt sauce, 53
 Drumsticks in tomato & mango chutney, 50
 Grilled chicken skewers, 62
 Marinated pesto chicken, 57
 marinades & glazes, 58–9
 Persian chicken skewers, 54
 Pirri-pirri chicken, 65
 Sesame chicken kebabs, 49
 Tandoori chicken, 55
 Thai drumsticks, 64
Blackened Cajun spiced chicken, 61
blue cheese & walnut salad, Chicken, 25
Braised chicken in white wine with capsicum & rosemary, 70
Braised chicken in wine & leeks, 88
breadcrumbs, 5
burger, Chicken bagel, 21

cacciatore with feta & black olives, Chicken, 71
Caesar salad, Smoked chicken, 28
Cajun spiced chicken, Blackened, 61
camembert filling, Chicken with cranberry &, 26
Canja, 17
cannellini beans, Chargrilled chicken salad with rocket &, 51
capsicum & rosemary, Braised chicken in white wine with, 70
capsicum & tomatoes, Chicken & rice with green, 85
carbonara, Chicken, 92
casserole, Chicken, mushroom & brown lentil, 75
celery filling, Creamy chicken &, 26
Chargrilled chicken salad with rocket & cannellini beans, 51
cheese
 Chicken & feta salad, 33
 Chicken, blue cheese & walnut salad, 25
 Chicken breast stuffed with spinach & feta, 105
 Chicken cacciatore with feta & black olives, 71
 Chicken mozzarella stacks, 30
 Chicken, semi-dried tomato & Gruyère jaffle, 26
 Chicken with cranberry & camembert filling, 26
 Gruyère chicken, 104
 Parsley & Parmesan crumbed chicken, 39
 Penne with sautéed chicken, asparagus & goats cheese, 87
Chermoula chicken, 60
Chicken, blue cheese & walnut salad, 25
Chicken, leek & sweet potato one pot, 74
Chicken, leek & tomato soup, 14
Chicken, mushroom & brown lentil casserole, 75
Chicken & artichoke pizza, 69
Chicken & asparagus stir-fry, 37
chicken & cabbage salad, Vietnamese-style, 23
Chicken & chickpea salad, 24
Chicken & corn jaffle, 26
Chicken & feta salad, 33
Chicken & mushroom soup, 11
Chicken & pasta bake, 72
Chicken & rice with green capsicum & tomatoes, 85
Chicken & sweet corn soup, 12
Chicken bagel burger, 21
Chicken breast stuffed with spinach & feta, 105
Chicken breast with balsamic relish, 102
Chicken cacciatore with feta & black olives, 71
Chicken carbonara, 92
chicken marylands, Stuffed 86
Chicken meatballs, 45
Chicken meatloaf, 80
Chicken mozzarella stacks, 30
chicken noodle soup, Asian, 7
Chicken Provençale, 67
Chicken rolls with creamy mushroom & peppercorn sauce, 107
Chicken san choy bau, 41
Chicken sandwiches with lemon mayonnaise, 19
Chicken sausage stir-fry, 46
Chicken, semi-dried tomato & Gruyère jaffle, 26
Chicken stir-fry with snow pea sprouts, 35
chicken stock, 5
Chicken stroganoff, 77
Chicken tarts with pumpkin, spinach & haloumi, 99
Chicken tikka kebabs, 56
chicken tortillas, Stir-fried, 36
Chicken wings marinated in soy, 52
Chicken with balsamic vinegar, 93
Chicken with cranberry & camembert filling, 26
Chicken with garlic & herb butter, 110
Chicken with peas & bacon, 91
Chicken with yoghurt sauce, 53
Chicken wonton soup, 16
chickpea salad, Chicken &, 24
chilli chicken, Coconut, 108
Chilli coconut chicken soup, 9
Chilli con pollo, 79
chilli stir-fry, Sweet, 42
Chinese braised chicken, 82
chive & lemon chicken, Roast, 109
Chunky chicken & vegetable soup, 8
coconut chicken soup, Chilli, 9
coconut chicken, Thai, 97
Coconut chilli chicken, 108
Coq au vin, 95
Coriander & lime chicken, 100
coriander pesto, Steamed chicken with, 100
corn fritters, Smoked chicken &, 32
corn jaffle, Chicken &, 26
coconut chicken soup, Chilli, 9
Cream of chicken soup, 15
Creamy chicken & celery filling, 26
Creamy chicken & zucchini soup, 13
Creamy chicken with tarragon, 38
Curried chicken with almonds, 76

defrosting, 4–5
Drumsticks in tomato & mango chutney, 50
drumsticks, Thai, 64

Easy chicken salad, 29

feta & black olives, Chicken cacciatore with, 71
feta & spinach, Chicken breast stuffed with, 105
feta salad, Chicken &, 33
freezing, 5
fritters, Smoked chicken & corn, 32

garlic & herb butter, Chicken with, 110
ginger, 5
ginger chicken, Tangy orange &, 43
ginger glaze, Lime &, 58
Glazed chicken legs, 90
glazes & marinades, 58–9
goats cheese, Penne with sautéed chicken, asparagus &, 87
Grilled chicken skewers, 62
grills & barbecues
 see barbecues & grills
Gruyère chicken, 104
Gruyère jaffle, Chicken, semi-dried tomato &, 26

haloumi, Chicken tarts with pumpkin, spinach &, 99
herb butter, Chicken with garlic &, 110
honey-glazed sweet potato, Chicken salad with, 20
Honey soy marinade, 58

Individual chicken & mushroom pies, 98

jaffles & sandwich fillings, 26

kebabs and skewers
 Chicken tikka kebabs, 56
 Grilled chicken skewers, 62
 Persian chicken skewers, 54
 Sesame chicken kebabs, 49

Lebanese chicken filling, 26
Lebanese chicken rolls, 31
leek & sweet potato one pot, Chicken, 74
leek & tomato soup, Chicken, 14
leek risotto, Baked chicken &, 73
leeks, Braised chicken in wine &, 88
lemon & chive chicken, Roast, 109
lemon mayonnaise, Chicken sandwiches with, 19
lentil casserole, Chicken, mushroom & brown, 75
Lime & ginger glaze, 58
lime chicken, Coriander &, 101
Lime steamed chicken, 96

Madrid chicken, 81
Mango chicken filling, 26
mango chutney, Drumsticks in tomato &, 50
mango, Satay chicken with, 103
marinades & glazes, 58–9
Marinated pesto chicken, 57
marylands, Stuffed chicken, 86
meatballs, Chicken, 45
meatloaf, Chicken, 80
Mexican marinade, 58
microwave defrosting, 5
Middle-eastern stir-fry, 47
mozzarella stacks, Chicken, 30
mushroom & brown lentil casserole, Chicken, 75
mushroom & peppercorn sauce, Chicken rolls with creamy, 107
mushroom pies, Individual chicken &, 98
mushroom soup, Chicken &, 11

olives, Chicken cacciatore with feta & black, 71
orange & ginger chicken, Tangy, 43
Orange & rosemary glazed chicken, 83
Oven 'fried' chicken, 84

Parsley & Parmesan crumbed chicken, 39
pasta bake, Chicken &, 72
patties, Spicy chicken, 22
peas & bacon, Chicken with, 91
Pecan-crusted chicken, 106
Penne with sautéed chicken, asparagus & goats cheese, 87
peppercorn sauce, Chicken rolls with creamy mushroom &, 107
Peppered chicken stir-fry, 40
Persian chicken skewers, 54
pesto chicken, Marinated, 57
pesto, Steamed chicken with coriander, 100
pies, Individual chicken & mushroom, 98

Pirri-pirri chicken, 65
pizza, Chicken & artichoke, 69
Portuguese chicken broth with rice, 17
pumpkin, spinach & haloumi, Chicken tarts with, 99

Redcurrant glaze, 58
rice, Portuguese chicken broth with, 17
rice with green capsicum & tomatoes, Chicken &, 85
risotto, Baked chicken & leek, 73
rissoles, Asian, 78
Roast lemon & chive chicken, 109
rosemary glazed chicken, Orange &, 83

salads
  Chargrilled chicken salad with rocket & cannellini beans, 51
  Chicken & chickpea salad, 24
  Chicken & feta salad, 33
  Chicken, blue cheese & walnut salad, 25
  Chicken salad with honey-glazed sweet potato, 20
  Easy chicken salad, 29
  Smoked chicken Caesar salad, 28
  Vietnamese-style chicken & cabbage salad, 23

san choy bau, Chicken, 41
sandwich & jaffle fillings, 26–7
sandwiches with lemon mayonnaise, Chicken 19
Satay chicken with mango, 103
sausage stir-fry, Chicken, 46
Sesame chicken kebabs, 49
skewers *see* kebabs and skewers
Smoked chicken & corn fritters, 32
Smoked chicken & spinach stir-fry, 44
Smoked chicken Caesar salad, 28
snow pea sprouts, Chicken stir-fry with, 35
soups
  Asian chicken noodle soup, 7
  Canja, 17
  Chicken & mushroom soup, 11
  Chicken & sweet corn soup, 12
  Chicken, leek & tomato soup, 14
  Chicken wonton soup, 16
  Chilli coconut chicken soup, 9
  Chunky chicken & vegetable soup, 8
  Cream of chicken soup, 15
  Creamy chicken & zucchini soup, 13
  Tortilla soup, 10
soy, Chicken wings marinated in, 52
soy marinade, Honey, 58

Spicy apricot chicken, 89
Spicy chicken patties, 22
spinach & feta, Chicken breast stuffed with, 105
spinach & haloumi, Chicken tarts with pumpkin, 99
spinach stir-fry, Smoked chicken &, 44
steamed chicken, Lime, 96
Steamed chicken with coriander pesto, 100
stir-fries
  Chicken & asparagus stir-fry, 37
  Chicken san choy bau, 41
  Chicken sausage stir-fry, 46
  Chicken stir-fry with snow pea sprouts, 35
  chicken tortillas, Stir-fried, 36
  Middle-eastern stir-fry, 47
  Peppered chicken stir-fry, 40
  Smoked chicken & spinach stir-fry, 44
  Sweet chilli stir-fry, 42
  Tangy orange & ginger chicken, 43
stock, 5
storage, 4–5
stroganoff, Chicken, 77
Stuffed chicken marylands, 86
Sweet chilli stir-fry, 42
sweet corn soup, Chicken &, 12

Tandoori chicken, 55
Tandoori marinade, 58
tarragon butter, Chicken with, 68
tarragon, Creamy chicken with, 38
Thai coconut chicken, 97
Thai drumsticks, 64
Thai marinade, 58
tikka kebabs, Chicken, 56
tomato & Gruyère jaffle, Chicken, semi-dried, 26
tomato & mango chutney, Drumsticks in, 50
tomato soup, Chicken, leek &, 15
tomatoes, Chicken & rice with green capsicum &, 85
tomato paste, 5
Tortilla soup, 10
tortillas, Stir-fried chicken, 36

Vietnamese-style chicken & cabbage salad, 23

walnut salad, Chicken, blue cheese &, 25
Whole chicken with tarragon butter, 68
wonton soup, Chicken, 16

yoghurt sauce, Chicken with, 53

zucchini soup, Creamy chicken &, 13

## INTERNATIONAL GLOSSARY OF INGREDIENTS

| | | | |
|---|---|---|---|
| capsicum | red or green pepper | fresh coriander | fresh cilantro |
| eggplant | aubergine | English spinach | spinach |
| zucchini | courgette | jaffle | toasted sandwich/waffle |
| tomato paste (Aus.) | tomato purée, double concentrate (UK) | tomato purée (Aus.) | sieved crushed tomatoes/ passata (UK) |

This edition published in 2003 by Bay Books, an imprint of Murdoch Magazines Pty Limited, GPO Box 1203, Sydney NSW 2001, Australia.

**Editorial Director:** Diana Hill **Editor:** Anna Sanders **Designer:** Annette Fitzgerald **Food Director:** Jody Vassallo **Food Editor:** Rebecca Clancy **Recipe Development:** Rebecca Clancy, Joanne Glynn, Eva Katz, Michaela Le Compte, Barbara Lowery, Justine Poole, Wendy Quisumbing **Home Economists:** Alison Adams, Laura Ammons, Michelle Lawton, Tracey Meharg, Kate Murdoch, Justine Poole, Margot Smithyman **Nutritionist:** Thérèse Abbey **Photographers:** Roberto Jean Francois, Reg Morrison (steps) **Food Stylist:** Michelle Noerianto **Food Stylist's Assistants:** Justine Poole, Michelle Lawton, Abigail Ulgiati **Food Preparation:** Michelle Lawton, Justine Poole
**Chief Executive:** Juliet Rogers. **Publisher:** Kay Scarlett.

The nutritional information provided for each recipe does not include any accompaniments, such as rice, unless they are listed in the ingredients. The values are approximations and can be affected by biological and seasonal variations in food, the unknown composition of some manufactured foods and uncertainty in the dietary database. Nutrient data given are derived primarily from the NUTTAB95 database produced by the Australian New Zealand Food Authority.

ISBN 0 86411 892 9.
Reprinted 2004. Printed by Sing Cheong Printing Co. Ltd. PRINTED IN CHINA.

Copyright© Text, design, photography and illustrations Murdoch Books® 2002. All rights reserved. No part of this publication may be reproduced, stored in a retrieval system or transmitted in any form or by any means, electronic, mechanical, photocopying, recording or otherwise without the prior written permission of the publisher.
Murdoch Books® is a registered trademark of Murdoch Magazines Pty Ltd.